insight text guide

Jarrod Sturnieks

High Ground

Dir. Stephen Johnson

Copyright © Insight Publications 2022

First published in 2022, reprinted in 2023, 2024.

Insight Publications Pty Ltd
3/350 Charman Road
Cheltenham VIC 3192
Australia
Tel: +61 3 8571 4950
Email: books@insightpublications.com.au

www.insightpublications.com.au

Copying for educational purposes
The Australian *Copyright Act 1968* (the Act) allows a maximum of one chapter or 10% of this book, whichever is the greater, to be copied by any educational institution for its educational purposes provided that the educational institution (or the body that administers it) has given a remuneration notice to Copyright Agency under the Act.

For details of the Copyright Agency licence for educational institutions contact:

Copyright Agency
Tel: +61 2 9394 7600
www.copyright.com.au

Copying for other purposes
Except as permitted under the Act (for example, any fair dealing for the purposes of study, research, criticism or review) no part of this book may be reproduced, stored in a retrieval system, or transmitted in any form or by any means without prior written permission. All inquiries should be made to the publisher at the address above.

A catalogue record for this book is available from the National Library of Australia

Dir. Stephen Johnson's High Ground / Jarrod Sturnieks

Jarrod Sturnieks asserts the moral right to be identified as the author of this work.

ISBNs:
9781922771209 (print)
9781922771216 (digital)

Cover design by Melisa Paredes

Printed by Markono Print Media Pte Ltd

contents

CHARACTER MAP

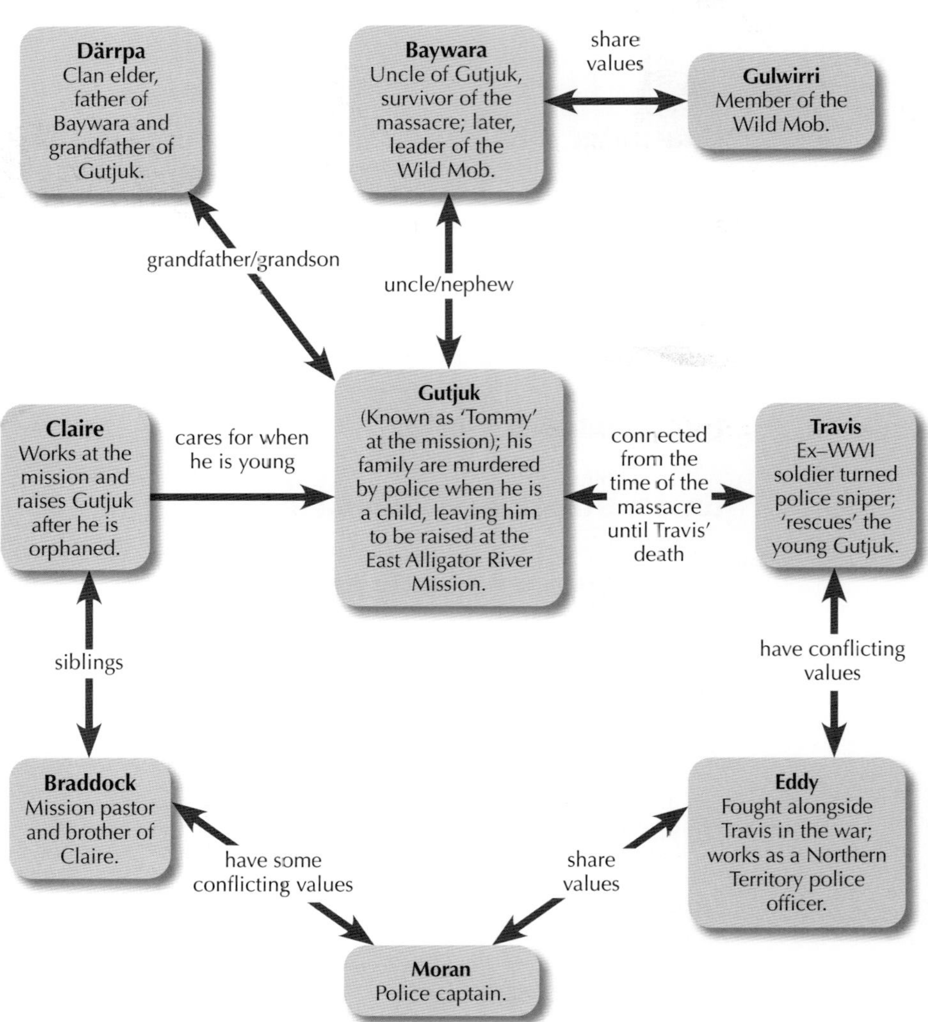

OVERVIEW

About the filmmakers

Director

Stephen Maxwell Johnson was born in the UK and grew up in Africa and Jamaica, the son of teachers who eventually settled in the Northern Territory to work at a school for First Nations students in Darwin.

Johnson has lived and worked in Arnhem Land for decades, learning about its history, including stories of First Nations massacres that were not taught in schools. He began his career as a television cameraman before developing his own production company based in the Northern Territory. Johnson honed his skills by directing several music videos for acclaimed band Yothu Yindi, winning a 1993 ARIA Award for Best Video for 'Djäpana'.

His debut film, the critically acclaimed *Yolngu Boy,* was released in 2001. It is a coming-of-age story about three teenagers navigating various challenges and temptations while finding themselves on the wrong side of the white man's law as well as the lore set by their own elders. As they trek through Arnhem Land and draw upon their childhood knowledge of bush culture, they reconnect with their roots and reclaim their identities. Made in collaboration with the Yolngu, the film was one of the first Australian feature films made with a First Nations lead cast. It was nominated for three awards at the Australian Film Institute Awards (now the AACTA Awards). Johnson took twenty years to develop his follow-up film, *High Ground,* which premiered at the Berlin International Film Festival in 2020. When it was released in Australia later that year, *High Ground* was a considerable critical and box-office success, grossing over $3 million locally.

Screenwriter

Chris Anastassiades began his career as a television writer before branching out into cinema, writing the screenplays for successful films such as *The Wog Boy* and *Hating Alison Ashley*. He also collaborated with Johnson on *Yolngu Boy*.

In preparation for the writing of *High Ground*, Johnson and Anastassiades spent considerable time with First Nations elders, listening to their stories and visiting various sacred sites, which enabled them to film the story in Arnhem Land and within Kakadu National Park.

Producers

A Yolngu man, Witiyana Marika was one of the founding members of the seminal Australian band, Yothu Yindi. In addition to his role as producer of *High Ground*, Marika was the senior cultural advisor and played the role of Grandfather Därrpa on screen. He also sings many of the traditional songs heard on the film's soundtrack, joined by his son Yirrmal, a successful musician in his own right. Marika refers to the collaboration between traditional owners and 'balanda' (non-Aboriginal) filmmakers as a 'both ways' film – a sharing of ideas and perspectives to bridge the two different cultures.

At the 2021 AACTA Awards, *High Ground* was nominated for ten awards: Best Film, Best Direction, Best Original Screenplay, Best Lead Actor (for both Simon Baker and Jacob Junior Nayinggul), Best Supporting Actor (for both Jack Thompson and Sean Mununggurr), Best Supporting Actress (Esmerelda Marimowa), Best Cinematography and Best Editing. The film was also named Best Film by the Film Critics Circle of Australia, who also awarded Best Director to Johnson, Best Screenplay to Anastassiades and Best Supporting Actor to Sean Mununggurr.

The film secured international distribution and was released in the US, Europe and Asia throughout 2021.

Synopsis

A purposefully confronting and unflinching depiction of Australia's Frontier Wars, *High Ground* portrays a discordant contrast between breathtaking landscapes and human brutality. In 1919 in Arnhem Land, we are introduced to a young First Nations boy, Gutjuk, who is learning the customs of his clan with his uncle, Baywara. Meanwhile, police officers surround the clan, following up on accusations of stolen livestock. The police are led by World War I veterans Eddy, who seems in command of the undertaking, and Travis, a sniper. The operation quickly spirals out of control, resulting in the senseless massacre of the entire clan. In a moment of unexpected rebellion, Travis also shoots two of his own men, horrified by their senseless and brutal killing of women and children. He also 'rescues' Gutjuk, who is then brought to a nearby mission run by Claire and her pastor brother, John. Travis' fellow police officers and their superior, Moran, are intent on denying the underlying cause of the violence, and Travis quits his position in disgust.

Twelve years later, Travis is reluctantly lured back to help hunt down a group of vigilantes known as 'the Wild Mob', a collection of First Nations warriors attacking homesteads and stations. The group is led by Baywara, who unexpectedly survived the massacre years earlier. Reunited with Gutjuk, now known as Tommy, Travis recruits him as a tracker, although he doesn't acknowledge their prior history. The two set off to find Baywara, followed by Eddy, who distrusts Travis and seeks his own revenge and the glory of capturing Baywara himself. Eddy travels with another police officer, Walter, who harbours his own suspicions and fears about Travis.

As all four men travel through the outback, tensions flare and threats are made. In spite of this, Travis and Gutjuk gradually learn to trust one another. As they finally encounter the Wild Mob, Gutjuk is reunited with his uncle and his grandfather, Därrpa. Another member of the mob, Gulwirri, seems to distrust Gutjuk and the men in her own group, seeing them all as weak and cowardly. Although Därrpa refuses to hand Baywara over to the police, he is anxious for peace and attempts an unsuccessful negotiation with Moran, both groups having their own conflicting ideas about justice.

Gulwirri and Gutjuk begin to foster a mutual respect and understanding after they rescue one another from peril. Gulwirri reveals her own reasons for being part of the Wild Mob: like Gutjuk, her family was killed and she was taken to a station, where she was exploited and abused. Her anger motivates her own sense of righteousness.

The police finally catch up to the Wild Mob. Travis, in another moment of miscalculation, shoots Baywara, provoking an additional round of retaliatory violence. In the fracas, Travis is shot by Gutjuk and apprehended by Eddy, returning to the mission in handcuffs, entirely disempowered.

Although his grandfather attempts to pacify his anger, Gutjuk returns to the mission for a final showdown. A fraught confrontation leaves Moran, Eddy and Travis all killed, the latter putting himself in danger to protect Gutjuk and Claire, redeeming him somewhat. Gutjuk, reclaiming his name and his identity, leaves the mission with Gulwirri.

Character summaries

Gutjuk

Gutjuk's name means 'hawk', although his totem is the crocodile. When we first meet him as a child he is eager to learn the ways of his clan. However, when his family is brutally murdered, he is taken to the East Alligator River Mission to be raised, where he is known as 'Tommy'. Twelve years later, he joins the pursuit of his uncle, eventually reuniting with some of his family. Gutjuk reclaims his identity and avenges the wrongs done to him.

Travis

Travis is a World War I veteran now working as a sniper for the Northern Territory police. Horrified by the unjust and indiscriminate violence he witnesses, he rebels by killing two fellow police officers and protecting a young boy, Gutjuk. Although he quits his position in disgust, he is brought back twelve years later to help track down a vigilante group. A reunion with Gutjuk forces him to confront his own guilt and complicity in the massacre, causing additional friction with his ex-colleagues and with Gutjuk himself.

Eddy

Another ex-soldier turned police officer, Eddy fought alongside Travis in the war, although they are clearly less than friends. Eddy takes pride in his military training and precision, but this doesn't stop him from losing control of an operation that ends with innocent blood being shed. Eddy reveals himself to be cruel, racist and unrepentant.

Moran

Moran is the police captain who oversees the police operations. He futilely attempts to uphold Australian Commonwealth laws on First Nations land.

John Braddock

The pastor at the East Alligator River Mission, Braddock accompanies the police in the operation that results in a massacre and is traumatised by what he witnessed. Despite his conscience and Christian values, he ultimately does little to improve the situation.

Claire

Braddock's sister Claire, who works at the Mission, raises Gutjuk after he is orphaned. She seems to genuinely care for the boy, continually fretting about the potential for more harm. The fact that she has learned the Yolngu language suggests she is different from some of her fellow Europeans.

Baywara

Gutjuk's uncle Baywara miraculously survives the massacre of their family and later leads a vigilante group known as the Wild Mob, who attack the homes of white settlers. Baywara's totem is the snake.

Därrpa

Därrpa is an elder of the clan, father of Baywara and grandfather of Gutjuk. Bewildered and concerned about the younger generation and their ideas about vigilante justice, Därrpa attempts to broker peace with Moran.

Gulwirri

A strong, warrior-like member of the Wild Mob, Gulwirri was previously kept as a station girl where she was exploited and abused. She lost her family to violence and harnesses her anger to fight back in resistance.

Walter

Walter is a Queensland police officer whom Eddy refers to as a 'half-caste bastard'. He occupies a space between the two cultures, yet is treated suspiciously by both sides. He has a history with Travis and the scars to prove it.

Bruce

A junior constable and Moran's nephew, Bruce brags of his rifle training and is brimming with misplaced enthusiasm to prove himself. Bruce is a minor character who plays a pivotal role in the final scenes, and he and Moran also serve as a contrast to Gutjuk and Baywara, who have a very different uncle-nephew dynamic.

BACKGROUND & CONTEXT

Terminology

Johnson collaborated with several clans and language groups in making the film and was motivated to tell a story from a Bininj and Yolngu perspective. Although the name of the clan is never explicitly mentioned in the film, Yolngu Matha is the language spoken by several of the characters. 'Yolngu' simply means 'people' or 'human' and 'Matha' means 'language'. However, by not identifying the particular clan depicted in the film, Johnson is unfortunately reminding us that this massacre could have been set anywhere in Australia.

Around 1919, the time period in which the film is initially set, there were many racist and distasteful terms used by Europeans to refer to First Nations people and several of these are heard in the film. Although they might need to be faithfully quoted to illustrate certain characters' ignorant and offensive perspectives, it is vital the appropriate contemporary terminology is employed when writing about the characters and their Country formally, objectively and analytically.

Firstly, it is essential to understand the distinction between the terms 'Aboriginal' and 'Indigenous', which are often used interchangeably and incorrectly. 'Aboriginal' has often been used to identify groups and custodians on the mainland of Australia and in Tasmania, creating a distinction between these populations and Torres Strait Islanders. However, 'Aboriginal' tends to lump many distinct groups into one simplistic collective. 'Indigenous' is a broader term that incorporates mainland First Nations people in addition to Torres Strait Islanders. Although a more appropriate term to use in place of 'Aboriginal' or 'Aborigine', some see this word as somewhat generic, as it is also used to describe flora and fauna. Further, it is a term that could be used anywhere in the world, not just Australia. It is also important to note that none of these terms were coined by First Nations people.

There has been a recent shift away from using terms such as 'Aborigine'. The preferred collective term used in this guide is 'First Nations' people, words chosen by many First Nations people themselves. 'First' reinforces their sovereignty, 'Nations' reminds us of the many distinct cultures that have always existed in Australia. Whether it be 'First Nations', 'Indigenous' or 'Yolngu', always capitalise these words in your writing. (Note that 'indigenous', lower case, is used only as general or broad adjective.)

Historical context

The Bininj and Yolngu have lived in the area known as Arnhem Land in the Northern Territory for centuries, and form one of the oldest and continuous living cultures on Earth. Arnhem Land is a region that consists of around 95 000 square kilometres in the north-eastern part of the territory. The name 'Arnhem' originally comes from a city in the Netherlands and was also the name of a Dutch ship that sailed into the Gulf of Carpentaria in 1623, although the Yolngu traditional names for these areas, one of which is Miwatj, predate European colonisation.

The Yolngu consist of several distinct clans who share cultural connections, each with their own dialects within the linguistic family known as Yolngu Matha. Sharing a rich culture with deeply entrenched practices, origin stories, food, music, art and dance, the Yolngu see themselves as coming from the land rather than simply owning or caring for the land. Their spiritual connection to their country clashed with European settlers with their very different, often imperious ideas about ownership.

Despite the rich history of the Bininj, Yolngu and all First Nations people, the Australian courts (that is, the British legal system) later codified the nation as terra nullius, a Latin term meaning 'nobody's land'. Such justification was used by colonialists the world over, dating back to the Doctrine of Discovery. This was a 1493 Papal decree aimed to justify Christian European explorers' claims on land they allegedly 'discovered'. What further motivated this pronouncement was the intention to promote Christian domination and superiority throughout the globe. Non-Christians were often considered less than human, further justifying a 'God-given' right to take land from them.

The unjust erasure of First Nations people and the sense of entitlement of many Europeans saw new settlers occupying lands with self-proclaimed sovereignty, and the original sovereignties are still not totally ceded today. This has resulted in a clash of legal systems where Australian Commonwealth law has attempted to ignore or trump First Nations' traditional laws or 'lore' – their own system of beliefs, practices and regulations passed down for generations by their ancestors.

Since Europeans colonised Australia, First Nations people have been dispersed or killed, in addition to suffering from the impacts of introduced diseases, particularly smallpox. This period can only be described in retrospect as a deliberate and callous dispossession and, at times, a systematic genocide.

The Yolngu were not unique in having fraught and often devastating interactions with European settlers from their arrival in 1788. As new European colonies emerged, so did acts of resistance from First Nations peoples across the nation defending their land, resulting in a series of conflicts known as the Australian Frontier Wars. These battles, beginning in 1788, are considered to have lasted up until the 1930s.

Although accurate figures are difficult to determine, there are estimates of between 20 000 and 60 000 First Nations people killed, in addition to the deaths of thousands of Europeans, as a result of colonial violence during this period. As knowledge about intergenerational trauma increases, it is clear that the effects of this dark chapter in Australian history are still being felt today.

Although a fictional rendering, the massacre that serves as a catalyst for the film's plot is based on real events that for many years were not widely reported or documented, and were subsequently ignored by Australia's Anglocentric education system. They have also rarely been depicted on screen, a fact that served as an impetus for the making of *High Ground*.

In recent years, the University of Newcastle has begun documenting frontier massacres across colonial Australia. This ongoing project strives to capture a more accurate record of events, including interactive mapping based on archival sources and empirical data – even firsthand witness testimony both from survivors and perpetrators. What is emerging is an often brutal, senseless pattern of violence.

One horrific act of violence, known as the Gan Gan massacre, has several parallels to the massacre depicted in the film. In 1911, more than thirty Yolngu men, women and children were slaughtered by mounted police outside of Darwin. This was done purposefully, a reprisal by police for the death of a white woman – a crime that was blamed on the Yolngu. There were two survivors of the attack who later relayed their eyewitness testimony of the senseless horror.

The violence perpetrated upon First Nations people has not been limited to murder; sexual assault of First Nations women was a common tactic employed in this period by some Europeans. Historian Henry Reynolds' book *With The White People* documents stations and settlements where 'Aboriginal women were preyed on by any and every white man whose whim it was to have a piece of "black velvet" wherever and whenever they pleased' (Reynolds 1990). Given that rape has been used as a weapon of psychological warfare in countless battles around the world, it is perhaps unsurprising yet still horrifying to know that numerous sexual assaults occurred during Australia's Frontier Wars, as Johnson's graphic and disturbing depiction of Gulwirri's rape in the film illustrates.

During the nineteenth and twentieth centuries, the rights and freedoms of Aboriginal and Torres Strait Islander people were curtailed and controlled by the state. Missions, often created and run by churches, in addition to stations and reserves, were established to effectively imprison First Nations people, converting them to Christianity and preparing them for a life of domestic servitude akin to slavery. These were often referred to as 'protectionist' policies, a paternal term that was used to sanitise or disguise the horrific abuse of human rights. The East

Alligator River Mission in *High Ground* was based on several similar outposts that took in First Nations children who had either 'lost' their families or had been forcibly removed from them.

At the time of the film's setting, Australia had emerged from its colonial period, was one decade on from federation and had just participated in World War I, fighting alongside its allies in Europe as the Anzacs (soldiers in the Australian and New Zealand Army Corps). This period helped form a unique national identity for many Australians of European descent, one that was beginning to detach from the 'motherland' of Britain. Many refer to this period as the actual 'birth of the nation', yet another concept that ignores First Nations sovereignty.

It is important to note that an estimated 1000 First Nations men fought among the Anzacs. Although they were expected to sacrifice their lives for Australia, they were not given the same benefits as other returned personnel. In fact, it was not until the 1967 referendum that First Nations people were even included in population censuses.

However, it is fair to say that all those returning from war undoubtedly experienced trauma that was not recognised in its day. With psychology and psychiatry still in its relative infancy, very little support was offered to combatants who had endured unspeakable brutality. As represented by Travis and Eddy in the film, these men were expected to carry on with their lives as normal, which saw their demons manifest in various ways.

GENRE, STRUCTURE & LANGUAGE

Genre

In many ways, the film fits the conventions of a traditional Western, a genre that emerged from the United States, a country with its own problematic and violent history. Westerns began as silent short films in the early twentieth century before the Hollywood studio system began making feature-length films in the 1920s and 1930s. Over the next few decades, this period, often referred to as 'the Golden Age of Hollywood', produced hundreds of Westerns.

The genre was dominated by formulaic films set on the American Frontier, or 'Old West', where European settlers began to colonise areas that were traditionally Native American reservations. As a result, conflict ensued between 'cowboys' and 'Indians' (the latter group described as such, despite being neither from the nearby Indies or India). In many of these films, Native Americans were often depicted stereotypically at best and as savages at worst, characterised as threats to law, order and morality.

In *High Ground*, however, Johnson subverts the usual Western tropes. Where white men on horseback were often portrayed as the noble, brave heroes in classic Hollywood films, Johnson has flipped the conventions to portray Europeans as the menacing, amoral antagonists, more savage than their counterparts. Still, Johnson's film shares many similar motifs to more conventional Westerns. The settings are familiar: harsh outback terrain, homesteads set ablaze in retribution, intimate conversations by campfire and galloping horses giving chase are all familiar features. At the core of most Westerns is the supreme battle of good over evil and the attempts to assert law and order in a tough, savage land. Johnson's film mixes many of these traditional elements with more modern, iconoclastic touches.

High Ground is also known as a revisionist Western, a subgenre that emerged in the US in the 1960s and 1970s. These films rejected the romantic depictions of frontier life in favour of realism, often blurring the lines between good and evil with more complex character development. This ambiguity portrayed many of the protagonists as flawed antiheroes and their counterparts as more sympathetic and less one-dimensionally villainous.

When Italian filmmakers began making revisionist films in the 1960s, this new subgenre was christened 'Spaghetti' Westerns. As such, when Australian movies such as *The Man from Snowy River* (1982) and several Ned Kelly films gained prominence, they were amusingly referred to as 'Meat Pie' Westerns. More recent Australian neo-Western films such as *Mystery Road* (2013) and *Sweet Country* (2017) were made by First Nations filmmakers with First Nations protagonists. Johnson himself refers to *High Ground* as a 'Northern' (for Northern Territory) rather than a Western.

Structure

In *High Ground*, Johnson adopts a mostly traditional, linear narrative that has one major jump in time. The first scenes serve as a prologue of sorts, with the majority of the film's action occurring twelve years later. There is a brief flashback at the climax of the film that returns to the establishing scenes featuring a young Gutjuk.

The opening shots of the film, wide shots of Nimbuwah, a sacred rock in Arnhem Land, are repeated before the final credits. The repetition of these shots serves to bookend the film and emphasise the motif of high ground. What appears as a sunrise in the opening credits is mirrored by a sunset in the closing credits, or potentially vice versa.

Visual language and film style

When analysing the film, you will need more than quotes to serve as textual evidence. In *High Ground*, much is communicated through visual language and the use of particular film techniques. As you view the film, consider the specific choices the director has made to create meaning and to convey a point of view. You also need to use the correct terminology (the precise metalanguage of film) in order to do this successfully.

Actors and acting

Although Australian-born, Simon Baker carved out a successful Hollywood career before returning home with the distinct purpose of telling meaningful Australian stories on film. In addition to acting in it, Baker also served as an Executive Producer on *High Ground*. The character of Travis is often laconic (speaking little), meaning that much of what Baker conveys with his character is through body language and facial expressions. He may serve as a proxy for white audiences, but Baker's Travis is a complicated, conflicted individual who is not entirely sympathetic.

Jack Thompson is an iconic presence on Australian screens, having appeared in numerous film and television shows dating back to the 1960s. Thompson also appeared as a police officer in Johnson's previous film, *Yolngu Boy*. Although often cast as a likeable Aussie larrikin in his earlier work, Thompson has evolved into more of a character actor in his later career, and imbues his role of Moran with a menacing authority, a man incredulous that not everyone shares his myopic worldview.

Perhaps even more explicitly villainous is Eddy, played by Callan Mulvey, who embodies his role with sinister and poisonous machismo. Mulvey smoulders and scowls with palpable disdain, operating as a formidable antagonist to Baker's Travis.

Johnson cast First Nations actors from the Arnhem Land area to make a closer connection with the story's setting. Witiyana Marika's Därrpa serves as a foil to Thompson's Moran and brings a quiet dignity and calm to the chaos. Jacob Junior Nayinggul and Esmerelda Marimowa both make their professional acting debuts in the film as Gutjuk and Gulwirri, respectively. Despite their lack of acting experience, they give performances just as compelling and moving as the more seasoned veterans in the cast and are arguably the moral core of the film. Even with little dialogue, the two actors command the screen through their physicality, projecting their characters' interiors often just in the mesmeric flashing of their eyes.

Camera

The landscape in *High Ground* can be seen as another essential character in the film. As such, the cinematography is a vital contributor to the story: beautiful, life-affirming, mysterious or foreboding, depending on the perspective. Very few of the shots are indoors, opening up this world and situating the audience directly amid the stunning wild beauty of the landscape.

Andrew Commis, the Director of Photography, alternates between aerial shots, extreme long shots, or wide shots of the vast terrain; handheld cameras for action scenes; and intimate, tight close-ups on the film's many characters. All of these shots contribute to capturing the unique Australian light, and form a sumptuous colour palette. Commis used as much natural light as possible when shooting, to strive for the most realistic and authentic viewing experience.

In the prologue of the film, as young Gutjuk learns the dances and totems of his clan, handheld camera shots, with their slightly shaky perspective, draw audiences into the immediacy of the moment. We watch Baywara from a child's perspective and share Gutjuk's wonderment. Commis' camera moves along with Baywara as he dances, immersing us in a private moment in this unique world.

The contrast with subsequent scenes is jarring and deliberately confronting. The peaceful lives of the clan are disturbed by images of galloping horses, an ominous sign. Audiences are placed into Travis' subjective viewpoint, watching the innocent women and playing children through a rifle crosshair, putting us in a very unsettling and disturbing position as the hunters.

For more intimate, dialogue-driven scenes, Commis prefers tight close-ups for proximity to the characters' anguish; here tensions are palpable. Commis also alternates between high and low camera angles to represent the powerful and the powerless, although these dynamics often flip. When seen from a low camera angle, characters appear confident, authoritative and strong. When shot from above (using a high camera angle), characters appear vulnerable and disempowered.

To mark the beginning of a new scene, particularly in a new location, Johnson often juxtaposes the action with shots of indigenous fauna: the many birds of Arnhem Land, green ants, snakes, goannas and crocodiles. When the narrative jumps ahead twelve years, Commis employs a tracking shot of a school of magpie geese in flight, to symbolically represent the swift passing of time.

Mise en scène

The term mise en scène extends beyond shot types and describes other elements of composition within the frame, referring to how and why the actors, and even their costumes and props, have been deliberately placed and lit within the setting. Essentially, you could freeze-frame any shot within the film and deconstruct the choices Johnson has made to deliberately position these elements in order to construct a deeper meaning. Several pivotal examples demonstrate the director's careful and considered arrangements.

The first is seen whenever Moran requests a formal photograph to document colonial life. Early in the film, when a crocodile is captured, Travis is placed in the centre of the frame, posing in a strong, slightly awkward stance with rifle in hand. On either side of him, two First

Nations men are in a squatting position. Even in a seconds-long shot such as this, we can see the unequal distribution of power between the men, and the superficial facade of machismo in white men who naively think they have conquered the natural world.

Later, when Moran commemorates his meeting with Därrpa, he places himself centrally in the formal photograph, seated as though a monarch on a throne, a proxy for the King himself. Next to him, Braddock and Claire stand uneasily, uncomfortably adjacent to the First Nations men in their traditional clothing. The contrast speaks of division and incongruity, with one group as natural and endemic as the surrounding trees while the other group seems entirely out of place (and out of line). Via a point-of-view shot through the lens of Moran's antiquated camera we see the action upside down, further reminding us that things are not as they seem.

Johnson's meticulous and revealing mise en scène is also utilised to full effect in the tense scene between Moran and Därrpa as they sit hopelessly deadlocked. A long shot, of Därrpa's clan to the left and Moran with the other European characters seated to the right, draws the eye to a massive chasm between the two groups.

Sound

Most films carefully balance the use of diegetic sound (that which originates within the world of the film; sounds that the characters themselves can hear) with non-diegetic sound (added for the audience's benefit; for example music scores and/or voice-overs). However, in *High Ground*, Johnson eschews a conventional Western soundtrack in favour of traditional First Nations music, sparse yet effective voice and percussion often performed by actor/producer Witiyana Marika and his son, Yirrmal Marika. Although technically non-diegetic (not being performed by the characters within the scene), the use of this music helps to immerse the audience in the world of First Nations people.

Marika's singing complements the visual beauty in addition to underscoring the narrative; the song cycle featured in the opening and closing credits tells a story about journeys. At times, Marika's voice heightens the intensity and often tragedy of what is depicted on screen. His haunting musicality at significant points in the film reminds the viewer of the devastating loss of culture, country and identity. The soundscape is also scattered with diegetic sounds of nature, the droning buzz of insects and the cacophony of birds seemingly upset by the intrusive sounds of boots clomping, horses galloping and guns firing.

Symbolism and motifs

The title phrase of the film itself is explicitly spoken by Travis when teaching Gutjuk to use his rifle: 'when you've got the high ground, you control everything'. Symbolically, this quote, repeated by Gutjuk later in the film, implies a moral superiority that other characters assume yet severely lack.

It is difficult to ignore the motifs of birds in the film, who literally possess a 'bird's-eye view' and perhaps occupy the highest ground of all. In the film's prologue, Baywara tells his nephew that Gutjuk means 'hawk' and we see one circling after his family has been murdered. Soon after, Därrpa learns of the massacre of his family via a school of squawking hawks. Johnson's drone shot of this news puts the audience in the unique position of the birds looking down on Därrpa. Throughout the film, we hear a variety of birds permeating the soundtrack, particularly in moments of peril. Many times, their squawks foreshadow and warn of ominous events on land.

There are other indigenous animals seen throughout, including a powerful sequence featuring a crocodile. Again, Johnson makes the choice to position the camera in such a way as to closely align the viewer with the animal's point of view as it is dragged from the water by Travis, as if the viewer is to sympathise with its plight. The later shots of this impressive creature bound by rope symbolise the attempts by colonial Europeans to 'tame' a savage land, striving for dominance not just over the animal world but over First Nations people themselves. This idea is even more thought-provoking given that Gutjuk's totem is the crocodile. However, any attempts to bind Gutjuk to the dubious moral code of the European characters is rendered futile. Ironically, Travis himself is seen as shackled and trapped later in the film, much like the doomed crocodile.

In addition to the focus on First Nations customs and spiritual practice in the establishing scenes, Johnson also blends shots of Christian symbolism, first seen when Braddock packs a Bible in his saddle sack before the massacre. This, in addition to several shots of the mission's open-air church standing precariously against the scrub, suggests an uninvited, incongruous Western presence on this land. In spite of Braddock's attempts to proselytise to First Nations people, he is mostly portrayed as a weeping mess of a man who is ultimately rendered ineffective. Reinforcing how out-of-place Christianity is on this land, the church is later burned down in a spectacular blaze during the film's climax, a powerful visual statement of resistance. The many fires seen throughout the story symbolise inflamed passions and even anger, but scenes of smoke and smouldering ashes hint at rebirth, new life and new possibilities.

Photography is another motif that lends itself to deeper contemplation. At various times, Moran insists on posing for or organising portraits for the 'official' record. Yet what is depicted on film rarely captures the reality of the situation. These photographs are awkwardly staged and deceptively constructed. This suggests that those representing the Commonwealth tried to control the narrative and present their flawed, biased and self-serving perspectives as 'truth'.

SCENE-BY-SCENE ANALYSIS

Chapter One (0:00:00)

Summary: *In the style of a prologue, a young Gutjuk learns the customs of his clan while police officers prepare their approach.*

The film opens with an establishing drone shot of Nimbuwah, standing elevated within pristine, almost prehistoric terrain. We then home in on a more personal setting: a young boy applying white ochre to his body and face in preparation for hunting a wallaby. This paint is considered sacred by the Yolngu and is used in several rituals and ceremonies. The soundtrack is deliberately subdued as Gutjuk and his clan members approach the animal carefully and quietly. The young boy misses his shot and is gently chastised by his father, Ngungki, who tells him to 'just watch and learn … one day your time will come'.

Gutjuk's uncle, Baywara, takes him aside to further instruct the boy in their traditions and customs, picking bush plums and performing the songs and dances of his clan, reminding his nephew, 'Your totem is the crocodile. Your name is Gutjuk, means hawk'. The innocence of Gutjuk is reinforced in these early scenes, as he is mostly portrayed quietly absorbing the lessons from his elders. Johnson uses several tight close-ups on the young boy as he observes these teachings, all of which will serve him well in his survival as an adult.

In these scenes, Johnson depicts First Nations people as literally treading lightly and purposefully, firmly establishing their knowledge of and clear respect for the land. This is juxtaposed with intrusive sounds of horses approaching, the first sign of a European presence lurking. This stark contrast already introduces a glaring divergence in how these two groups will be portrayed for much of the film.

Baywara and Gutjuk are startled by two First Nations men in Western clothes on the run from 'station men' after killing a cow. They are given refuge for one night – a decision which has devastating consequences for all.

As children frolic in a waterhole and Gutjuk's mother, Wak Wak, prepares food, the women of the clan ponder why Gutjuk is 'in such a hurry to grow up', firmly yet fondly asserting that 'he needs to learn his place'. Meanwhile, police officers arm themselves with rifles and bandoliers (cartridge belts) as though preparing for battle. Despite the perceived differences in the two groups, both concede, in separate conversations, that they 'don't want any trouble'. Yet there is an ominous sense of foreboding. The First Nations hunters are now being hunted.

Q How is First Nations culture established in these scenes?

Q Which qualities of the adult Gutjuk are already hinted at or foreshadowed here?

Chapter Two (0:08:00)

Summary: *The police lose control of the operation, resulting in a bloody and senseless massacre.*

The pretence of avoiding 'trouble' is immediately contradicted by trigger-happy members of the police impatiently asking, 'What are we waiting for?' Here, the characters of Eddy and Travis are introduced and already their duelling power dynamics are at play; Eddy is the leader with a clear strategy, Travis the sniper on higher ground seemingly part of his chain of command. Yet Travis is already questioning the operation, watching his fellow police officers in the distance and rhetorically asking impatiently, 'What are you doing?'

Johnson's point-of-view shots via Travis' rifle crosshairs are particularly chilling. As members of the clan innocuously bathe, play and hunt for food, they are being systematically targeted. Their traditional spears and weapons are no match for the police rifles. Baywara's ironic proclamation that 'it's our land, we should fight' foreshadows his character's later motivations of resistance, rebellion and pride.

A lurking Eddy, shot from a low camera angle, inadvertently steps on a branch and startles Gutjuk who sounds the alarm and sets off a chain of bedlam and violence. Baywara is shot first before the police start firing wildly, targeting the women and children. These scenes are, by design, confronting, brutal and tragic, reinforced with shots of white cockatoos and black crows crowing and squawking mournfully. A hawk seemingly transports news of the massacre to Därrpa, Baywara's father and Gutjuk's grandfather. An extreme wide shot is employed here, a bird's-eye point-of-view shot as Därrpa emerges from a cave to question this report of danger – 'What are you saying? What are you telling me?' – before he takes flight himself, running towards his slain family.

Gutjuk survives the first round of violence and his mother firmly grabs him by the wrists, pulling him into the waterhole, showing him how to breathe underwater using reeds. Her protective, maternal instinct saves her son but she is soon hunted down and shot herself.

The reactions of the European men vary. Some treat the massacre as sport ('Did I get her?'), while others are appalled: Braddock (the pastor who accompanies the police) vomits and cradles the dead, crying and praying to himself. In an unexpected moment of rebellion, Travis shoots one of his own: the man who had killed Gutjuk's mother. He kills a second policeman, one who has already been speared through the chest, a response that could be seen as either merciful or treacherous, or both. 'Look away!' he instructs Braddock as he fires. Eddy and Travis are already depicted as adversaries, pulling weapons on one another in a brief stand-off that will build to a full reckoning later in the film. Travis is clearly an outlier here, as he finds Gutjuk hiding beneath waterlilies and responds with a protective, almost paternal embrace of the young boy rather than shooting him.

Q What is the significance of the first rifle crosshairs focusing on Eddy and the other police officers?

Q What is the significance of many of the clan being shot in the back?

Chapter Three (0:14:30)

Summary: *East Alligator River Mission Outpost; the aftermath of the massacre; fractured loyalties.*

At the nearby mission, we are introduced to Braddock's sister Claire, who senses something terrible has occurred. 'What happened?' she asks, alarmed. Travis is unable or unprepared to answer her. She is handed a traumatised Gutjuk to care for, reinforcing the expected caretaking role of women. Yet in these scenes, Claire's hostility is festering and she later slaps Travis for his complicity in the tragedy.

Braddock is the only one of the men outwardly displaying remorse, while Eddy is more concerned with getting the official story straight. 'What'll we tell Moran?' he asks. Although we are not yet introduced to their superior, Johnson alludes to a wider hierarchy of command. Eddy deflects any responsibility, attempting to scapegoat another member of their unit and to subtly influence Travis to follow suit. Travis calls out Eddy's fake remorse by reminding him, 'you fired first', defiantly refusing to lie. 'You can tell Moran whatever you want. I'm not stickin' around for it', he tells Eddy dismissively as he rides away from the mission.

As Därrpa cradles the bodies of his slain family, Johnson introduces the idea of retaliation, symbolically represented by a fiery red blaze. This could also hint at a rebirth of sorts; unbeknown to the audience, Baywara has miraculously survived.

Q Is Travis' departure motivated by guilt or disgust?

Chapter Four (0:20:00)

Summary: *Twelve years later; although Travis has moved on, the past catches up with him.*

A time jump in the narrative is signified with a tracking shot of a school of magpie geese in flight. Johnson introduces this section of the film with another aerial drone shot of a rock, this time a smaller rock formation than that in the opening shot of the film. Travis has traded his sniper duties for crocodile-hunting.

Key point

Here we are introduced to Moran, who takes a photograph of Travis' catch, arrogantly and ignorantly declaring that 'it is the responsibility of those who make history to record it'. Although Moran is documenting an official record of colonial life, he tries to control the narrative and his lens is myopic, entirely missing the big picture.

Moran, with Eddy in tow, has come to ask Travis' assistance in capturing the Wild Mob – a vigilante group (led by Baywara) Moran refers to as 'a bunch of black bastards wreaking havoc'. This conversation is set by a campfire, a motif Johnson returns to throughout the film and a site at which intimate and important conversations will occur. Without any hint of irony, Moran declares that the mob 'crossed a line' by killing a white woman, seemingly oblivious to the massacre of innocent women and children by his own men.

Moran's motivation for wanting to capture Baywara seems less to do with justice or punishment and more to do with suppressing the truth of the massacre of Baywara's people years before. 'I don't need to tell you what happens if this Baywara gets a voice', he tells Travis, who seems relieved at the possibility of the real truth emerging. 'The truth's a funny thing', replies Moran in veiled threat, reminding Travis that his bullets ended up inside two of his fellow police officers. Travis can hardly contain his contempt and reluctance at the prospect of pairing up with Eddy yet again.

Meanwhile, the Wild Mob continue to burn down local homesteads. An adult Gutjuk faces their wrath but is released when he reveals himself to be Baywara's nephew. In the afterglow of blazing flames, uncle and nephew are briefly reunited.

Q How does Johnson depict the Wild Mob? Does this match Moran's judgements of them?

Chapter Five (0:26:25)

Summary: *Travis agrees to take Gutjuk on the journey to track down Baywara; both men conceal their true motivations and intentions.*

In an open-air church at the mission, Braddock addresses a small congregation that includes his sister and Gutjuk.

Key point

Here Braddock reads Isaiah 5:8 – 'What sorrow for you who buy up house after house and field after field, until everyone is evicted and you live alone in the land'. His carefully selected reading seems to critique the very idea of colonialism.

Gutjuk, now known as Tommy, is seen working on the mission, dressed in European clothing and speaking English. Braddock refers to him as a 'good boy', a remark meant in earnest but with patronising connotations.

Eddy arrives at the mission and disrupts the peace with threats against both Gutjuk and Travis. Although he restrained himself in the previous scene, his true colours emerge and it is clear he has not changed in the past decade. Travis and Eddy's adversarial relationship is reignited as they tussle in the dirt.

Travis agrees to take Gutjuk along as a tracker instead of teaming with Eddy; the more insidious implication is that Gutjuk will be used as a 'bait' to lure Baywara. As Gutjuk pleads with Travis to keep his uncle safe, Travis is unable to offer much reassurance: 'I'll do my best. That's all I got.' His inscrutable facial expressions don't reveal any real sentimentality about being reunited with Gutjuk. Yet his guilt and shame are clearly still simmering under the surface, as he tells Eddy, 'I won't make the same mistake twice.'

Travis is not the only one disguising his real motivations. Gutjuk tells an elder his agreement to track Baywara was not entirely sincere, suggesting that he was misleading them when he states, 'They went for it.' Gutjuk sends word to Baywara that they are coming for him, suggesting that Gutjuk's loyalties still remain with his clan, and setting up a reckoning and revenge that is long overdue. Travis sees through

Gutjuk's ruse, telling Eddy, 'If his mind's on that, maybe he won't see what I'm doing'. The conflicting loyalties and motivations are firmly established and lay the foundations for the tensions that will inevitably arise.

As Gutjuk readies to leave, Claire addresses him in his language. 'It's their war not yours', she says, tenderly embracing him. 'Don't trust them.' She is right to doubt the men. When Travis and Gutjuk leave, Eddy ominously follows them, aware of Travis' past disloyalty.

Q Why is it significant that Claire is the only European character who has learned to speak Yolngu Matha?

Q Characters in this scene distrust each other. What do they each fear? How does this create and build tension?

Chapter Six (0:34:00)

Summary: *Travis and Gutjuk traverse the land, slowly building trust with each other; conflict with Eddy escalates.*

Travis and Gutjuk's expedition is more than a geographical excursion, it's also a slow journey of trust-building. When asked his name, Gutjuk replies 'Tommy, Sir' – a response that could read as rote, deference or withholding. As they arrive at a recently deserted campsite, the contrast between the two men is striking. Travis is nervous, jumpy and breathless, grasping his rifle out of fear. Gutjuk, shot from a low camera angle, looks calm and comfortable among the goannas, snakes and green ants.

Travis and Gutjuk gradually reveal more about themselves. Gutjuk spots a circling hawk and reveals to Travis his true name. Travis teaches Gutjuk to use his gun, telling him, 'When you've got the high ground, you control everything' – a loaded statement that speaks symbolically of morality as much as it speaks concretely of strategy. Yet Gutjuk remains tight-lipped when Travis asks for the location of his uncle.

Back at the mission, we are introduced to Walter, a character who occupies a unique space between cultures. As a 'half-caste' police officer from Queensland, Walter's position is one that was common yet controversial in colonial Australia. Moran praises Walter as an asset, but he is seen by First Nation elders as a traitor: a 'bad fella ... kills his own'. Not wanting to relinquish any glory for Baywara's capture, Eddy pursues Travis, reluctantly taking along Walter yet dismissing his tracking skills as 'blackfella mumbo jumbo'. Walter tells Eddy he's apprehensive, having met Travis previously and still bearing the scars to prove it. 'Our doubts are traitors', Eddy tells him, dismissing any caution or nervousness as weakness. Yet this bravado can't fully disguise Eddy's fears, since he knows full well Travis' shooting prowess.

Travis reveals to Gutjuk that he and Eddy have a history that predates the massacre, as both fought in World War I, where Eddy was Travis' spotter. When Gutjuk offers Travis bush plums, he prefers the ration-like tinned meat he ate during the war. Gutjuk's perceptive retort is that he 'thought the war was over'. Here Johnson reminds us that although World War I has ended, Australia's Frontier Wars are still very much ongoing. As the two men start to relax around one another, gradually forming a bond, Gutjuk tries to explain why Baywara turned out the way he did: 'If he had a chance, he'd be a different kind of man.' Travis replies with 'I'm not sure anyone gets to choose', suggesting that he believes in the capacity of external forces to shape one's destiny.

Gutjuk takes Travis' gun and lurks around Eddy's campsite, yet he's not noticed by Eddy, who is boasting of his own 'precision' and 'sound military planning' as an ex-soldier. Johnson's framing of Eddy in these scenes reinforces his villainous qualities. In uncomfortably tight close-ups, Eddy's eyes dart back and forth, almost making direct eye contact with the audience in an unsettling and menacing way. Suddenly, Walter pulls his weapon on Travis nearby, resulting in a tense showdown between all four men, each with their own underlying motivations and resentments. In this uneasy exchange, Walter reveals that Moran's orders were that 'no one comes back': yet another ambiguous statement that could be read as permission to kill or as a reminder that Travis' earlier betrayal can never be forgiven. Travis, unarmed, manages to de-escalate the situation, asserting that 'the plan's changed … I'll do things my way', and grabbing Walter's guns. Although the inevitable showdown has been delayed for now, Travis keeps Eddy and Walter in his crosshairs as they depart, a reminder that their reckoning is still to come.

Q What are the conflicting motivations of each of the four men here?

Chapter Seven (0:49:30)

Summary: *The Wild Mob; Grandfather's country; Cutjuk's conflicted loyalties.*

Just as Eddy and Walter depart, Travis is surrounded by the Wild Mob pointing their spears at him. Gutjuk's facial expressions are intriguing at this juncture: he maintains eye contact with Travis except for a split second of downcast doubt, suggesting a modicum of sympathy. Yet Gutjuk says nothing, still keeping his true feelings hidden. A little humour lightens the mood as the men mock Travis' looks, reminding the audience that the Wild Mob are far from bloodthirsty killers.

Tensions continue to flare between Eddy and Walter. Again, tight close-ups of Eddy's sinister facial expressions reinforce the evil bubbling under the surface. Eddy loads his gun as children happily play nearby, reminding us of his role in the massacre and the possibility of more deaths to come. When Walter has the audacity to question Eddy's contributions in the war, he takes exception to being belittled and launches into a tirade that borders on sadistic, threateningly reminding Walter that 'Travis is the nice one'.

Key point

As they walk through smouldering terrain, Baywara tells his nephew that Gutjuk is finished with the mission – 'your life starts now' – with the smoky ashes hinting a rebirth and a turning point.

As they head towards Grandfather Därrpa's country, Gutjuk shows the first sign of conflicted loyalties, concerned about Travis' welfare in the hands of the mob. Baywara reassures his nephew that he could have killed Travis if he wanted to, again reinforcing that the Wild Mob have their own sense of justice, one far more moral than Moran had suggested.

Somewhat surprisingly, Därrpa greets Baywara with anger for bringing Travis along as a bargaining tool: 'This madness stops now.' Därrpa reminds us that his people have their own justice system that Baywara needs to reckon with, and refuses to hand his son over to Europeans and their punitive ideas of justice. Travis, knowing firsthand the bloodlust of the police, is unable to assure Därrpa that his family will remain safe. In a gesture of good faith, Travis' gun is returned to him but, ascertaining his relative powerlessness and futility, Därrpa asks to speak to Travis' boss instead.

We also learn more about Gulwirri in these scenes. Although Gutjuk is clearly intrigued by her, Baywara tells him she is 'too wild that one'. She is portrayed as warrior-like, strong, defiant and focused, yet is shown walking slightly apart from the men, indicating that she is not entirely the warrior they are. Later, she chastises Gutjuk for being a 'mission boy pretending to be a man'. Gulwirri's scorn isn't reserved just for him; she calls all the men 'weak' and 'cowards' for trusting in Gutjuk and Travis. Her defiance is intensified when she is framed from a low camera angle, from where she claims the high ground.

Q How does Därrpa advocate for conflict resolution?

Q How does this clash with Baywara's ideas of justice?

Chapter Eight (0:58:47)

Summary: *Därrpa approaches Moran with hopes of making peace.*

Moran insists on another formal photograph to commemorate the meeting, placing himself centre stage as though on a throne as he commands everyone present to follow his orders. Johnson's use of mise en scène reinforces the divisions between the two groups, in addition to the awkwardness and forced formality of the situation.

The tension here is almost tangible. The First Nations characters, in white ochre paint, begin the meeting with a traditional ceremony which seems to bewilder Moran. He attempts to explain the British monarchy, preposterously pointing to the Commonwealth Coat of Arms on his hat. This is met with indifference by Därrpa and stealth mocking by Gutjuk who chides that it 'makes him think he's boss'.

It's clear that both groups claiming sovereignty will result in deadlock. As Johnson portrays them facing one another during these discussions he juxtaposes this with extreme close-ups of each patriarch's face. The massive chasm between them seems insurmountable. Moran refuses to negotiate, reminding them of his duty to uphold Commonwealth laws. Därrpa (through Gutjuk's translation) pushes back: 'This is my law. It comes from the soil. From Mother Earth. My law is perfect. Consistent.'

Key point

Although devoid of any violence, this scene is almost as tense as the massacre itself, portraying a reckoning where cultures, hostilities, mistrust and misunderstandings all intersect.

Moran is not used to being challenged, his facial expressions revealing his incredulousness and impatience. He claims to believe in balance ('makarrata' is restoring balance) but won't budge an inch, insisting everyone needs to follow Commonwealth laws and taking exception to Därrpa's claim to 'my country'. Därrpa throws Moran's hypocrisy back at him, reminding him they are still waiting for their own justice for the massacre. Here, Moran deflects somewhat, conceding that he's merely an officer of the law, a cog in a much larger machine.

Eddy relays news that the Wild Mob have just attacked another station, resulting in two more casualties. Moran uses this as an excuse to call off the negotiations – tellingly, just as his authority and command was slipping. Därrpa and his clan depart, interestingly taking many of the First Nations men and women from the mission along with them.

Q Claire remains relatively marginalised and silent during the negotiations. What do her facial expressions and body language reveal?

Chapter Nine (1:08:45)

Summary: *Gulwirri is assaulted by a group of white men; she seeks vengeance.*

As Travis prepares to leave, Claire's disdain rears its head once more. Still reeling with disgust for Travis' complicity and concerned that more bloodshed is inevitable, she confronts him: '… you're just going to let it happen?' Travis yet again conceals his true intentions, telling her, 'I'm not gonna make it easy for them' but offering no further reassurance.

Braddock's gun is stolen from the mission and given to Gutjuk who uses it to save Gulwirri from a sexual and physical assault by two white men. This is the first example of First Nations people taking Western weapons and turning them back on their oppressors, yet it won't be the last. Although Gulwirri's guttural screams are particularly disturbing, she refuses to play the role of helpless victim. In a definitive reversal of power, she savagely attacks and kills her rapists, and rescues Gutjuk. Interestingly, she doesn't need a gun to reclaim her power. 'Don't watch', she tells Gutjuk, challenging the idea that it is women who are squeamish. Her command echoes the very same sentiment Travis used in his moment of rebellion in the initial massacre, when he told Braddock to 'look away'. As directed, Gutjuk turns his head to shield his gaze from witnessing even more bloodshed than he already has.

As they clean up, Gutjuk attempts to impress Gulwirri by demonstrating his shooting skills, only for her to bluntly dismiss him: 'You think like a white man.' Although they journey on without speaking to each other, two magpie geese fly above them in tandem, hinting that perhaps they are not so dissimilar after all.

Q How is Gulwirri's violence different from the violence we have already seen?

Chapter Ten (1:14:30)

Summary: *More misunderstandings lead to more violence.*

Again we see First Nations people in point-of-view shots through Travis' crosshairs, echoing the scene of the first massacre, but this time it won't be a surprise attack. Gutjuk warns his uncle of more men approaching yet Baywara seems unperturbed. Defiant as ever, Baywara boldly states, 'we'll send back ghosts'. Initially refusing to take his nephew's advice, he is sternly told by Gulwirri to listen and trust Gutjuk. Loyalties and power dynamics have shifted considerably within the mob, which infuriates Baywara. As he pulls a spear on his nephew in order to make a point, Travis, misinterpreting the body language from afar, shoots Baywara. As in the early scenes there is unnecessary bloodshed by a waterhole, based on compulsion and miscalculation. Although Travis possesses the higher ground here, ironically it gives him less perspective, not more.

Eddy and his men use this as a sign to surround the entire mob and start shooting, the diegetic sound of squawking birds signalling more danger. The mob's spears are an effective match for the gunfire, resulting in casualties on both sides. Travis kills Walter, who was seconds away from shooting Gutjuk. Far from being grateful, Gutjuk instead fires his rifle directly at Travis for his perceived betrayal. When Gutjuk roars, 'It was you!' he is unequivocally blaming Travis for his uncle's death. Yet it's somewhat unclear whether he also remembers Travis from his traumatic childhood, which served as the catalyst for the latest wave of violence. 'It was you!' could also be interpreted as a revelation of recognition.

Unsurprisingly, Eddy has no sympathy for the wounded Travis. He half smirks as he mocks his former colleague: 'We need to talk about your choices, mate', a low camera angle portraying Eddy asserting his short-lived dominance. Travis is handcuffed and returned to the mission. In a private conversation – one of few filmed indoors – Moran tells Travis they are both 'bad men' but are the foundation their civilisation is built upon. This is a scathing observation and it is somewhat surprising that Moran expresses an indictment of the Australian Commonwealth justice system and colonialism more broadly. Stripped of formality and pretence, Moran's true colours are revealed as he justifies his own immorality. This time, he takes a spontaneous photograph, eager to capture Travis shackled and humiliated. 'Whatever made you think you could change who you are?' Moran asks, interpreting Travis' attempts to redeem himself as disloyal. The scene ends with close-ups of a seething but silent Travis.

Q How is this massacre similar to the initial one? How is it different?

Chapter Eleven (1:20:30)

Summary: *Gutjuk receives conflicting advice; he contemplates his next move.*

Aerial drone shots of the terrain deceptively suggest peace, yet the camera homes in on Gutjuk carving a spearhead from rocks. It is apparent that his fury has not been satiated. As he crafts a new weapon, we are transported back to his childhood via a flashback to a young Gutjuk looking admiringly at Baywara's spears. This is the only time Johnson disrupts the linear narration of the film, reinforcing a full-circle moment for Gutjuk.

Därrpa again watches in bewilderment at how the younger generations deal with their anger. Concerned about potentially losing more family members, he warns Gutjuk about following Baywara's path in letting his anger consume him, advising him to instead listen to Mother Earth for guidance. Although Gutjuk half-nods, it doesn't halt his purpose and he is still carving the spearhead by the campfire that evening.

Here, Gulwirri joins him and drops the harsh resentfulness of earlier scenes, a shift in mood that is symbolised by the warm, glowing light from the fire. She matter-of-factly confides in Gutjuk; just like him, her family was also killed and she spent her childhood in servitude and slavery on a station. It is a poignant, tender moment that succinctly justifies Gulwirri's driving force. Her advice – to harness his anger and 'keep fighting' – directly contradicts Därrpa's. Again, Gutjuk absorbs the advice but it is still unclear which direction he will ultimately take.

Back at the mission, Claire continues to fret about more violence brewing. As she nurses Travis' wounds, she has slightly softened her contempt for him, yet her main concern lies with Gutjuk's welfare.

Key point

Eddy asserts his supremacy unequivocally by telling her that you 'can't share a country, Claire'. Just like Moran, Eddy reveals his true colours. This blatantly racist viewpoint that was always beneath the surface is finally laid bare for all to see.

Gutjuk, not waiting to be stalked and killed, approaches the mission along with Gulwirri. At a nearby campsite, he mercifully lets two white men free and burns their bullets, suggesting that he doesn't want any more bloodshed than is necessary.

Q How are Gutjuk's and Gulwirri's traumatic experiences similar?

Q Why is it significant that Gutjuk is carving his own weapons and abandoning bullets?

Chapter Twelve (1:28:30)

Summary: *The inevitable reckoning; delayed justice.*

The blazing church symbolises a shift in power and authority. As Gutjuk approaches the mission, he turns his gun on Moran and demands that Travis be brought out to face him. Gutjuk and Gulwirri's embracing of rifles symbolises a reversal here, as the weapons of the colonisers are turned back on them.

As he pulls the gun on Travis, Gutjuk finally reveals that he knows Travis was among those who killed his family. Johnson's high camera angles reinforce the subversion, with Moran and Travis on their knees, powerless and vulnerable. This tense exchange is framed almost from Gutjuk's point of view, the camera positioned over his shoulder, looking down the barrel of his rifle. Here, Gutjuk takes exception to being called

Tommy and reminds them all of his true name. His sense of identity is finally reclaimed.

Travis manages to overpower and disarm Gutjuk. Yet when Moran tries to shoot Gutjuk, Travis instead fires at Moran, marking at least the third time Travis has 'saved' Gutjuk. As a furious Eddy arrives, he screams at Travis, 'You care more about this black piece of shit than you do about yourself', proving himself racist and wrathful until the very end. As the two war veterans face each other in one final stand-off, Eddy is killed by a surprise bullet fired by Claire. This is the first time she is deliberately shown dressed in pants instead of her usual skirts, reinforcing her rebellion against traditional gender roles.

As Gutjuk embraces Claire, Travis notices Moran's nephew, Bruce, about to fire on the pair and puts himself in the line of fire instead.

Key point

Travis dies, holding Gutjuk's hands and saying the young man's true name to him. Close-ups of their firm grasp and tearful facial expressions reinforce their complicated but undeniable bond.

In another unexpected parallel, Gulwirri makes eye contact with Claire. In this moment the two share an unspoken kinship as women who are marginalised but finding their own forms of empowerment and retaliation. Gutjuk and Gulwirri flee the mission together as the mournful but affirming traditional music underscores their departure. The penultimate shot tracks an ascending hawk in the sky before Johnson returns to the aerial shot of Nimbuwah from the beginning, with the sun now setting in the background.

Q Has Travis redeemed himself?

Q Is this a hopeful ending?

CHARACTERS & RELATIONSHIPS

Gutjuk

Key quotes

'One day your time will come …' (Ngungki, 0:03:50)

'I thought the war was over.' (0:44:10)

'You're finished with the mission. Your life starts now.' (Baywara, 0:52:00)

In retrospect, the opening scenes of a young Gutjuk are heartbreaking in their depictions of his innocence and childlike wonderment, given the cruel fate that awaits him and his family. The boy has a keen sense of purpose, eager to learn his culture and 'in a hurry to grow up', as the women of his clan observe. Although he is still quite young, his destiny seems assured.

In contrast, when we meet an adult Gutjuk at the East Alligator River Mission he seems stuck in arrested development. 'Tommy' rings the mission bell, dutifully attends the church services, is referred to as 'helping out' at a nearby station and deferentially addresses others as 'sir'. With his culture, identity and family unjustly ripped from him, he moves slowly and cautiously, and speaks almost in a monotone. Both Claire and Braddock are even dismissive of his ability to serve as a tracker, since he is so far removed from what he once knew. Although attired in the same hat, shirt and pants as the white Australian characters, the similarities are only superficial. He's out of place, suspended in a location and a situation that he had no say over.

Yet Gutjuk has clearly not forgotten his kin. A brief reunion with his uncle as he helps contain a blaze set by the Wild Mob serves as a catalyst for an overdue re-examining of his priorities and purpose. Over the course of the film, Gutjuk reclaims his identity and eventually avenges the wrongs perpetrated upon him and his family. As such, Gutjuk disproves the harmful colonial belief that forcibly removing First

Nations children from their families would result in positive outcomes, showing instead that bloodlines run deep, regardless of time and place.

Mirroring Travis' concealment of his motives, Gutjuk keeps his goals hidden, agreeing to serve as a tracker for Travis but intending to lead him into a trap instead. What follows is a masterful game of deception and one-upmanship that inevitably leads to more violence. Gutjuk is shrewder and smarter than Travis realises, knowing that trust needs to be earned rather than freely given.

However, the burgeoning relationship between Gutjuk and Travis complicates things considerably and makes it harder for both men to keep their focus on their initial strategies. Gutjuk gradually learns to trust Travis, revealing his true name and sharing bush plums. Later, Gutjuk pleads with his uncle that Travis is 'a good man' and is concerned about what will become of him.

The final scenes portray a more animated, aggressive and assertive Gutjuk. Inspired by Gulwirri and her unapologetic defiance, this Gutjuk is significantly different from the naive, scared little boy from the prologue, and worlds away from the compliant 'mission boy'. All of Gutjuk's suppressed anger comes to the forefront in a true blaze of glory. Smeared in warpaint, bandoliers across his chest, he arms himself with spears and a rifle to avenge his family's deaths. Yet unlike his merciless enemies, he demonstrates true empathy and humanity in holding Travis' hand as he dies.

Key point

Although it is Travis who teaches Gutjuk strategy and the importance of having 'the high ground', it is clear which character possess the moral superiority, the real 'high ground' in the film. Gutjuk is one of the few characters who doesn't kill another, despite having the means, justification and opportunity.

Travis

Key quotes

'I won't make the same mistake twice.' (0:30:25)

'When you've got the high ground, you control everything.' (0:39:45)

'I'm not sure anyone gets to choose what kind of man they're gonna be.' (0:44:40)

'… he's a good man.' (Gutjuk, 0:52:20)

In many ways, Travis is a difficult character to examine. While lacking villainous qualities, he is not a traditional hero either, despite some noble and courageous acts. One could generalise that Travis is typical of white Australian men from his generation: raised to value machismo and discouraged from showing vulnerability. Respected, even feared, for his excellent marksmanship, Travis has been recruited to use his skills for unspeakable horrors both in wartime and, ironically, during 'peace time' back home. Consequently, as his own morals are tested and compromised, he seems unable or unwilling to process his traumas. Although he exhibits visible signs of unease and revulsion regarding the violence he has faced and perpetrated, men of his ilk were certainly not encouraged to speak about their feelings or reveal any signs of weakness.

Travis has the luxury of fleeing the scene of the first massacre without any reckoning or punitive consequence. He has no ties that bind; no family we know of; no romantic entanglements or robust friendships. When it becomes clear that Eddy and his superiors do not share Travis' dismay about the massacre, he simply washes his hands of the situation and leaves. 'You can tell Moran whatever you want', he tells Eddy, 'I'm not stickin' around for it.' His departure is part cowardice, part denial, and reeks of privilege.

This does not mean Travis isn't principled, as he clearly possesses his own innate sense of right and wrong. His split-second decision to turn on his colleagues, even killing them, is born from his disgust at their cruelty and bloodthirstiness. This reaction is impulsive, showing that

Travis is hardwired to act on instinct. Although he doesn't stay to see justice done, he refuses to continue his complicity in the carnage. When asked to toe the line, he tells Eddy he will not lie about what happened.

Travis has moments in which his inner world is revealed to the viewer but mostly he's inscrutable. When reunited with Gutjuk, he makes no mention of their past connection, provides no insights into his motivations and only reveals as much information to Gutjuk as he deems necessary. When Travis does speak, he mostly focuses on facts, not feelings. His laconic, even curt, manner creates tension, uncertainty and conflict.

Therefore, Travis' inferred guilt can only truly be measured by his actions. When he tells Gutjuk, 'I'm not sure anyone gets to choose what kind of man they're gonna be', it's in direct reference to Baywara's decisions, yet speaks volumes about his own direction in life. Drawn unwillingly into the Frontier Wars and other people's agendas, he seems to be frustrated, even disappointed in himself, swearing he 'won't make the same mistake twice'.

When Travis is captured, first by the Wild Mob then chained and imprisoned by Eddy and Moran, he almost accepts his fate. He doesn't argue, fight back or try to escape. This may suggest that he knows punishment is just, and is a form of penance that is inevitable for him. In the concluding moments of the film, he again makes a split-second decision. By sacrificing his own life for Gutjuk, he has found the only real way to at least partially redeem himself.

Key point

Although Gutjuk refers to Travis as 'a good man', this description only tells half the story. The film doesn't always depict Travis sympathetically or heroically, despite his virtues. He is a deliberately challenging and perplexing character.

Baywara and Därrpa

Key quotes

'My uncle … he was my teacher. I think if he had a chance, [he'd] be [a] different kind of man.' (Gutjuk, 0:44:30)

'This madness stops now.' (Därrpa, 0:54:00)

'We need to make peace.' (Därrpa, 0:57:30)

'They send men and we'll send them back ghosts.' (Baywara, 1:15:00)

The differences between Därrpa and his son Baywara are vast. Although both have a deep connection to their culture, they diverge in their beliefs about justice and conflict resolution. Baywara's sense of righteousness stems from his own victimisation, miraculously surviving the massacre that killed many family members. Refusing to live in terror, he forms a vigilante group that instead terrorises settlers, an empowering yet renegade way of reclaiming his power and dominion over the land. Gutjuk sympathises with his uncle's situation, lamenting that he never 'had a chance' to be anything 'different'. Baywara's anger is portrayed as somewhat justifiable, or at least understandable. His violence is primarily a means of sending a stern message to those encroaching on his country. This bellicose (aggressive or warlike) drive of Baywara's is foreshadowed early on, when he tells a young Gutjuk in the film's early scenes, 'I strike like lightning', assuming a warrior pose.

Yet Baywara is astute enough to sense what he's up against. In a moment of rare vulnerability, he returns to his father's country for assistance, saying, 'Father, you said if I was in trouble you would help me.' Unperturbed by his father's rebuff, he carries on with his calling, warning that he will 'send back ghosts' should anyone try to stop him. Although his death is shocking, in the context of the Frontier Wars and the odds stacked against First Nations people it seems tragically inevitable.

All of this agonises Baywara's father. Därrpa's prudence and worry is entirely reasonable given how many of his family had already been killed.

A cautious yet commanding presence, he is bewildered by the Wild Mob and their terror campaign of perceived recklessness. Underpinning his reservations are his paternal love and protective instincts. This is clearly seen in the aftermath of the massacre as he stumbles upon the bodies of his family, mourning 'my children! My family! Who did this to my family … my beloved daughter?'

Later, Därrpa bemoans his son's untapped potential: 'Baywara could've been our greatest teacher. But he lost all that to his anger.' Despite his inherent wisdom failing to penetrate his son, he attempts to pacify his grandson before he, too, makes the same mistakes. To Därrpa, the answers lie all around them; he tells Gutjuk, 'You need to listen to the wind, listen to Father Sky. Listen to Mother Earth.'

Därrpa serves not only as a contrast to his own son but a foil to Moran. The two patriarchs sit eye to eye during their negotiations but their philosophies could not be more divergent. Where Moran demands respect, tries to dominate and refuses to consider shifting his limited and self-serving worldview, Därrpa listens respectfully, appeals for fairness and aims to 'restore balance'. Even after being dismissed and patronised by Moran, Därrpa remains a calm presence in a world of chaos.

Eddy

Key quotes

'… nothing gets the job done like sound military planning.' (0:46:40)

'… Travis is the nice one.' (0:51:25)

In the aftermath of the massacre, Eddy bemoans the 'chaos' that unfolded, more concerned with losing control than with the loss of life. An ex-soldier turned police officer, he prides himself on precision and is quick to attack anyone who dares to challenge or defy him. There is evidently no love lost between Eddy and Travis. Although they fought together during the war, Eddy is keen to clarify that 'he's not my mate'. Underlying Eddy's dislike and distrust of Travis is a sense of insecurity and possibly envy. He erupts when Walter has the audacity to question his contributions in wartime, reminding him that as a spotter Eddy actually 'didn't do any of the shooting himself'. Travis is the one revered for his shooting prowess, leaving Eddy seething with bitterness about his role as second fiddle.

The pursuit of Baywara is nothing more than unfinished business for Eddy, an opportunity to settle scores. He explicitly discloses this: 'Don't tell me it doesn't haunt you', he says to Travis, 'that you don't want it off your back?' This explains why he follows Travis, not trusting his former colleague but also not wanting to relinquish the glory of Baywara's capture. Eddy revels in the violence, menacingly relaying to Walter his experience of being a spotter and watching people die before him: 'You watch as the head explodes. You see a mist of blood, the dead eyes.' As his bloodlust intensifies, so does all pretence that his role as a police officer is anything to do with law and order. Eddy's shameless racism is on display for all to see, such as when he tells Claire, 'you can't share a country', or when he admonishes Travis for defending Gutjuk: 'You care more about this black piece of shit than you do about yourself. God knows why.' Eddy embodies the worst of postcolonial Australia, a hostile and sadistic brute who only succeeds at revealing his own ugly heart.

Moran

Key quotes

'It's the responsibility of those who make history to record it.' (C:21:50)

'I didn't come here to negotiate.' (1:03:40)

'You know how a civilisation's built, son? Bad men. Bad men doing bad things …' (1:19:00)

Through his insistence on staging formal photographs at each juncture, senior police officer Moran shows that he is more concerned with maintaining the facade of dignity and nobility than actually living it. Although he tasks himself with upholding Commonwealth law, his ideas of justice are subjective and hypocritical. Despite boasting of being 'duty bound' to the King, he resorts to immoral and unethical tactics to have his way, confessing to Travis that 'there are other ways to handle this situation'. By any means necessary, Moran is intent on suppressing the truth of the massacre, displaying more concern about Travis' rebellion than the blood shed by his own orders.

When given an opportunity to hear the valid concerns of Därrpa, asking for justice for his immeasurable loss, Moran is callously indifferent. This quickly builds to incredulousness when he doesn't receive the respect and genuflection he assumes his position will grant him. Stubborn and contemptuous, Moran is inadvertently contributing to his own demise by choosing domination over reconciliation.

While attempting to maintain a public image of authority and formality, in private Moran reveals that the Commonwealth consists of 'bad men doing bad things. Clearing the way for the others to follow', an opinion he boldly divulges with a modicum of glee. In paternally calling his fellow police officers 'son' and even recruiting his own nephew to help police the outback, Moran is preparing for even more men 'to follow' his wicked ways. His wishes would ensure a continued cycle of systemic oppression and brutality in postcolonial Australia.

Gulwirri

Key quotes

'Too wild that one.' (Baywara, 0:52:40)

'You're all weak. Cowards. Cowards who talk when they should fight.' (0:58:00)

'I know how it feels to be beaten. To feel like nothing. That's why you have to stay angry and keep fighting. Your anger is all you have.' (1:23:40)

The first scenes of Gulwirri portray her as aggressive and hostile, supporting Baywara's judgement that she's 'too wild'. Although she fights along with the Wild Mob she seems to be the only woman and distances herself from the men at times. Opinionated, she's not afraid to voice her dissent and reprimands the men around her when she feels they are misguided. Initially, she is wary of Gutjuk and his perceived allegiance with Travis, but gradually she learns to trust him.

We eventually learn what fuels her rage. In a tender moment, she speaks to Gutjuk about her past. Working at a station when she was 'just a little girl', she was exploited by her boss who 'thought he owned me' and 'gave me to his men'. Like Gutjuk, her family was killed. When she is attacked and sexually assaulted by a group of white men, her response is to turn their savagery and viciousness back at them, single-handedly murdering them all in revenge. Gulwirri represents resistance, although she clearly takes no pleasure in what she has to do.

Claire

Key quote

'It's their war not yours. Don't trust them.' (0:32:20)

As the male characters strategise and scheme, Claire's only concern is about Gutjuk's welfare. At every turn, she poses questions about him that demonstrate her attachment and apprehension, even if she is often dismissed. Despite her obvious care for Gutjuk, it is interesting that her initial rage about the massacre seems to stem from Braddock having to witness it. She slaps Travis, furious that her 'brother's a mess' as a result of the botched operation.

Claire is an empathetic and maternal figure, contrasting with the brutality that surrounds her. When many of the European characters around her resort to violence and racist epithets, she speaks the Yolngu language and embraces Gutjuk with real tenderness. Therefore, it comes as a surprise to see her take up arms in the final moments of the film, killing Eddy before he can cause any more damage. Her moment of bravery and revolt echoes Travis' own earlier rebellion, as both characters turn on 'their own'. Their core sense of morality trumps any imposed allegiances.

THEMES, IDEAS & VALUES

Postcolonial Australia

Key quotes

'What sorrow for you who buy up house after house and field after field, until everyone is evicted and you live alone in the land.' (Braddock, quoting the Bible, 0:26:30)

'It's their war not yours.' (Claire, 0:32:20)

'See this crown on the badge? That represents the King. The King of the British Empire. And that is the law that I am duty-bound to uphold.' (Moran, 1:02:50)

'Can't share a country, Claire.' (Eddy, 1:26:00)

In many ways, Johnson's film is a critical indictment of colonial and postcolonial Australia and the uncomfortable truth underpinning European settlement – it was stolen land never ceded. The film reverses the conventions of classic Western films in that the settlers here are certainly not portrayed as 'the good guys' fighting to uphold morality in a savage, ungodly land.

In addition to the uneasy race relations, colonial life presented many other challenges for settlers: establishing settlements on hot, dry, unforgiving land and attempting to bring a European culture and sensibility, uninvited, to a very different part of the world. The mission is portrayed as slightly successful in that there are buildings erected, a makeshift church built and Christian services in place. Yet these are easily and quickly destroyed in the final scenes of the film, reinforcing their precarious standing. There are also First Nations people dressed in European clothing, who seem to live at the mission. Yet, if the character of Gutjuk is any indication, they are not necessarily there by choice. At times, the European characters seem ill at ease, nervous, ill-equipped to live on this land or even just inappropriately attired for the harsh Australian climate. None of these characters seem particularly happy with their lot in life, each struggling in different ways, unable to recognise their own responsibility for this misery.

Johnson's focus on the pristine Australian landscape – one the First Nations people know, understand and respect – also builds a strong case that these settlements, stations and churches are incongruous. In addition to their presence, their buildings, introduced livestock and religion, the colonisers bring European weapons of war, leading to devastating consequences.

Moran represents the Australian Commonwealth, a role he seems particularly proud of. Throughout the course of the film, he is portrayed as ridiculous at best, cynical and insidious at worst. When meeting Därrpa, an attempt at negotiation that came about in good faith with sincere intentions from the elder, Moran's response is breathtakingly arrogant and hypocritical. Wearing a military uniform that seems ludicrous in the Australian outback, he points to the crest on his hat, saying, 'See this crown on the badge? That represents the King.' He challenges Därrpa's use of the phrase 'my country' and haughtily expects the First Nations people, with their own entrenched justice system dating thousands of years, to follow his laws – the King's laws. He is impatient with and bewildered by Därrpa and his people, and completely ignores the fact that their laws predate his by thousands of years.

Moran also attempts to assert his authority in defusing Gutjuk's ire in the final confrontation, expecting his title to protect him. 'I am the second most senior officer', he boasts. Gutjuk immediately disarms him, literally and figuratively: 'Shut up old man', he spits back. When Moran is shot, there is very little sympathy for him.

It is important to note that throughout the film, Moran also makes mention of 'eyes down south', 'the higher-ups' and 'the Commissioner' to explicitly reference a larger system that he is one small part of. Although Johnson's film is set in a specific area of Australia, the implication is that these attitudes and this type of sanctioned violence was widespread at the time.

Although Moran refers to the Wild Mob derogatorily as 'myalls' (an indigenous shrub or tree), colloquially and ironically the term was also used by First Nations people to refer to ignorant, unwanted strangers. Eddy represents the arrogant and racist ideas embodied by many early settlers; propagating dominance, displacement and destruction. He perceives his skills as superior to 'blackfella mumbo jumbo' and shows no remorse for the innocent lives shed by his hand. When he tells Claire that 'you can't share a country', he is justifying his use of violence as the only way to assert his self-appointed hegemony. His death is likely to be met with relief by audiences, not only as the removal of the villain from the narrative, but as the symbolic eradication of a hateful and toxic presence in this beautiful land.

Yet Eddy is not the only one who embodies such racist attitudes; other European characters refer to First Nations people using slurs such as 'black bastards' and 'coons' throughout the film. This reveals the blatant disregard, ignorance and outright mockery some colonialists exhibited regarding First Nations cultures. Such language goes beyond ignorance to actual dehumanisation. This sense of superiority makes it easier to perpetuate more violence, as seen when Gulwirri is raped by a group of laughing white men. There is a sense of satisfaction for the viewer when they are brutally killed by her.

Key point

With Johnson portraying so many of the racist and arrogant European characters meeting violent ends, he is not only drawing on the Western genre convention of the triumph of good over evil, he is also critiquing and condemning the noxious, racist attitudes that some early settlers possessed.

Johnson doesn't paint all of his characters with the same critical brush. Claire is arguably the only European character who shows any real empathy, compassion and tenderness. Her brother, Braddock, displays emotion, outwardly grieving the loss of innocent children, but he's rendered too traumatised to be effective. Claire is more productive and useful, as symbolised when the first shot of her in the film sees her applying a bandage to an injured First Nations elder.

In slapping Travis, Claire is the only character who challenges and chastises him for his role in the massacre. In the film's final scenes, she takes the law into her own hands and adds to the momentum of restorative retribution. It is her finger that pulls the trigger on Eddy and ends his reign of terror, at least temporarily. It is also not insignificant that Claire has taken the time to learn the Yolngu language and she is even thanked by Därrpa for taking care of Gutjuk as a child. Her sole motivation over the course of the film seems to be a genuine, maternal concern for the mission residents and in particular for Gutjuk's wellbeing. As such, her character constitutes a more gentle, open-minded and moral depiction of postcolonialists.

Travis represents a more complicated response to colonialism and the trail of devastation left in its wake. A man who fought for his country in World War I only to return home and perpetrate more violence, he clearly wrestles with guilt. Although he is referring to his own complicity in the massacre when he uses the word 'mistake', by extension one could interpret this as a reference to Travis wrestling with his conscience about European settlement also being a mistake. His insubordination in instructing Eddy, 'tell Moran the plan's changed. From now on I'll do things my way', represents Travis' rejection of Commonwealth laws and the idea that they rule supreme.

Justice and revenge

Key quotes

'... they crossed a line. They killed a white woman.' (Moran, 0:23:10)

'Makarrata. Restore balance.' (Därrpa, as translated by Gutjuk, 1:04:55)

'You stand for justice? ... Then you give us our justice for the man who killed my family. This didn't start with my uncle. This started with you. You want us to respect your law? Give us our justice.' (Därrpa, as translated by Gutjuk, 1:06:00)

There is a running discourse throughout *High Ground* about justice, with much of the conflict stemming from the fact that each character has very different ideas about what is just. The desire for retribution snowballs over the twelve-year time frame, beginning with police officers looking to punish those who stole a cow, which in turn leads to an act of indiscriminate brutality perpetrated on the innocent, which subsequently breeds even more desire for revenge. The film portrays a vicious circle, complicated by intersectional and overlapping resentments.

One could argue that this cycle of injustice began with colonisation itself, the initial invasion and dispossession of First Nations people from their sovereign land. Although the film never explicitly references this as the fundamental wrong fuelling all subsequent conflicts, the idea is always bubbling beneath the surface. By hunting down two First Nations men accused of killing livestock from a nearby station, the police hark back to the biblical idea of 'an eye for an eye'. This ancient form of justice effectively rationalises measure-for-measure violence, although the punishment endured here far outweighs the crime. Those massacred in the film had nothing to do with the inciting crime of killing a cow and were essentially in the wrong place at the wrong time.

These heartbreaking scenes of mayhem and carnage explicitly and provocatively outline what systemic and state-sanctioned injustice looks like at its worst. The initial massacre and its repercussions hang over these characters like a dark cloud. Yet it is also a useful gauge to measure all subsequent acts of violence in the film, weighing up each deed to ascertain which is worse and which is warranted. Not all acts of violence in the film are unjustified.

This idea of retribution recurs throughout the film, although the punishment dispensed varies considerably. Baywara represents another form of payback in his embrace of vigilante justice. Leading the Wild Mob to terrorise European settlers, he sees value in being feared instead of living in fear. Although a victim of the massacre, he refuses to be victimised. Moran categorises the mob as 'wreaking havoc, killing livestock, burning stations'. While we are never shown Baywara's version of events, it is implied that these are not random acts of indiscriminate violence but a form of planned revenge. Ironically, Moran decides that the Wild Mob have 'crossed a line' by resorting to murder, never once considering the underlying provocations and his own complicity in murder.

Baywara also reckons with his own father's ideas of right and wrong. Därrpa represents the desire for restorative justice, believing that the anger and violence embodied by his son is 'madness'. Instead, the elder yearns for peace, even insisting on meeting with Moran in an attempt to 'restore balance'. This is a completely different approach from the vengeful motivations of his son and the mob. Därrpa refers to his ideas of justice and law as 'perfect' and 'consistent', and suggests that they 'cannot be undone', but his wishes are not fulfilled, with Moran completely oblivious to the fact that First Nations people have had their own justice system in place for thousands of years. In his discussions with Moran, Därrpa uses the Yolngu term 'makarrata' to represent the idea of restorative justice.

Key point

Johnson himself identifies 'makarrata' as the core idea of the film, the need for unity and acknowledgment of wrongdoing before any progress or reconciliation is possible. In the negotiations with Därrpa, Moran stubbornly refuses to take any responsibility and, as a result, more unnecessary bloodshed follows.

Gulwirri is another character who takes matters into her own hands by murdering her tormentors. This is where the ideas of justice and revenge start to blur: she sees the two concepts as one and the same, and audiences are encouraged to agree with her. While the violence she resorts to is primal and terrifying, her victims are far from blameless and it's difficult to argue that they are undeserving. Gulwirri's anger motivates her; 'You have to stay angry', she tells Gutjuk. 'Keep fighting. Your anger is all you have.' Her 'fight' is one of the more justified and principled conflicts depicted in the film.

Occurring soon after the slaying of Gulwirri's rapists, the deaths of Moran and Eddy in the denouement of the film are designed to elicit complex responses from viewers. While not endorsing or advocating violence, the film is offering a resolution and a relief of sorts when evil is punished, warning of the consequences if more traditional forms of justice are denied.

In the series of deaths seen in the closing moments of the film, almost a domino effect of consequentiality, Travis is also killed. He takes the bullet that ends his life when he steps into the line of fire to protect Claire and Gutjuk. This does not necessarily undo or allow viewers to forgive his past sins, but it is portrayed as a step in the right direction towards restoring balance.

Violence and trauma

Key quotes

'(*crying*) Seventeen dead. It's children …' (Braddock, 0:17:00)

'You know what a spotter does? You don't just find the target. You confirm the kill. You watch as the head explodes. You see the mist of blood, the dead eyes.' (Eddy, 0:51:00)

'You know how a civilisation's built, son? Bad men. Bad men doing bad things …' (Moran, 1:19:00)

Closely interrelated with the theme of justice, violence infuses each frame of the film. Johnson forces his audience to confront Australia's bloody history in all its unflinching and uncomfortable ugliness. Sometimes this is explicitly witnessed on screen; in other scenes, characters are reeling from violence, fleeing from violence or eager for more bloodshed.

Key point

Although the violence in *High Ground* is purposefully horrific, the intent behind it varies depending on the character and situation, and it is important to recognise the distinctions Johnson is drawing.

While the director condemns some acts of violence, particularly the initial slaughtering of innocent women and children, he appears to condone its use in certain instances, such as when Gulwirri murders her attackers. However, he stops short of explicitly advocating violence. If not necessarily endorsing it for the purposes of revenge, he is at least sympathetic towards those characters who resort to violence when they have few options left. Such moments of aggression can serve as catharsis, relief and even perceived justice for both the perpetrators and the viewing audience.

One impact of violence alluded to is the inevitable but sometimes invisible trauma that results from witnessing or experiencing such savagery. The adult Gutjuk, known as 'Tommy' on the mission, initially presents as a stoic, considerate and amiable young man, showing no outward signs of suffering, grief or anger. Yet once back in the outback and faced with more violence, his traumatic past catches up with him and we see him attempting to reconcile himself to the aftermath of losing his family and culture. It is not until the final minutes of the film that his anger emerges. 'You killed my family!' he screams at Travis, 'Say it!'

This trauma is not always concealed. In the moments after Gulwirri's vengeful attack on her rapists, she is visibly disturbed and disgusted by what she has been forced to endure, yet again. Both she and Gutjuk survived childhood trauma only to face it again, figuratively and literally, as adults. 'I know how it feels to be beaten, to feel like nothing', she confesses to Gutjuk, in a rare moment of vulnerability. Her trauma fuels her rage and, tragically, this trauma never seems to end. As she stands by and witnesses the deaths of Moran, Eddy and Travis, she shares eye contact with Claire as if to express the incredulity and utter exhaustion of having to constantly endure the folly of men.

Another subtle illustration of trauma lies in the deliberate choice to characterise Travis and Eddy as World War I veterans. As Anzacs, ordered to kill on behalf of their country, they inevitably endured and perpetrated horrific violence, returning home, like so many others, damaged and shell-shocked. These men were expected to return to regular life and simply move on as though their trauma didn't exist. Eddy and Travis portray drastically divergent postwar experiences. Where Travis is seemingly repulsed by violence and plagued with guilt, Eddy seems to revel in bloodshed, perpetrating the same violence he undoubtedly experienced fighting in Europe.

When attempting to lure Travis back into the fold and join the hunt for Baywara, Eddy brings up the massacre, saying to his former colleague, 'Don't tell me it doesn't haunt you … that you don't want it off your back?' Yet this is far from a sincere moment of remorse. Whereas Travis is clearly haunted by guilt, Eddy is only haunted by a job left incomplete.

The film also depicts the shifting nature of power through violence, represented by Gutjuk and Gulwirri appropriating modern weapons and turning them back on their oppressors. European characters are portrayed as confused and indignant about this change of events, expecting First Nations people to remain passive and terrorised. 'What are you doing pointing a gun on a whitefella, Tommy?' one of Gulwirri's rapists asks. Moran shares this disbelief when Gutjuk points a rifle in his face, visibly taken aback by the audacity of Gutjuk turning his weapon against him. These shifts present a fascinating and satisfying subversion where the powerless find ways to empower and liberate themselves. However, it's important to note that Gutjuk and Gulwirri also destroy (rather than use) some of the bullets, and don't completely abandon their traditional weapons either.

Trust and loyalty

Key quotes

'… we got through the war by sticking together. Trusting each other. Now we'll get through this together.' (Moran, 0:25:00)

'Don't trust them.' (Claire, 0:32:20)

'Travis has no sense of duty, no sense of loyalty. That's a problem.' (Moran, 0:33:30)

Another consideration that complicates the characters' decision-making is the idea of loyalty and the dilemma of who to trust. This shifts and changes over the course of the film as individuals are pulled in different directions; trust is broken and loyalties are frayed. Some see virtue and valour in unity, others exert their will via independence and autonomy.

In the aftermath of the massacre, Eddy's first priority is for the surviving police officers to get their stories straight. As such, he demands an allegiance, telling Travis that they must 'act as a unit'. Valuing 'precision' in his line of work and having fought alongside Travis in the war, when unity was essential for survival, Eddy sees any dissent as disloyal. When Travis leaves the mission in disgust, Eddy seems to take it personally. Later, Eddy attempts to get him back onside, flattering Travis by telling him it was Eddy's decision to recruit him. Moran also reminds both men that 'we got through the war by sticking together. Trusting each other.' His appeals fall on deaf ears and the two war veterans remain adversaries throughout the film.

Travis is more loyal to his own innate sense of right and wrong than to an externally imposed value system, which explains his instinctual impulse to kill his fellow police officers. Yet clearly his colleagues and superiors don't see his actions as virtuous. Moran uses the massacre as leverage, threatening to expose the truth of Travis' rebellion by asking, 'How did two whitefellas end up with your bullets in them?' Although Moran needs Travis, benefiting from his skills as a sniper, he doesn't trust him, telling Eddy that 'Travis has no sense of duty, no sense of loyalty. That's a problem'. Later, when Travis kills Walter and is handcuffed to a bed frame as punishment, Moran calls him a 'mad dog' and threatens to hang him for his treachery. To Moran, Travis' disloyalty is the greatest crime of all: 'You break my heart, son.'

The building of trust between characters is made all the more complicated when each of them keeps their true feelings and intentions hidden. When Travis is reunited with Gutjuk as an adult, he makes no mention of their past connection, nor does he reveal how the operation to track down Baywara will unfold. Travis is impenetrable and enigmatic, which unsettles Gutjuk. He doesn't know whether to trust Travis but he's also in no position to refuse him. In turn, Gutjuk engages in some deception of his own. While agreeing to accompany Travis, he reveals to an elder, 'they went for it', suggesting his acquiescence was an act of trickery that concealed his own equally inscrutable intentions to warn his uncle and lead Travis into a trap of sorts. Yet Travis senses that Gutjuk 'knows more than he's letting on', intending to lure the boy as 'bait' to serve his own agenda. Johnson builds layer upon layer of duplicity that will inevitably be exposed.

Initially, Gutjuk refuses to tell Travis his true name, but eventually the two form a bond of sorts, opening up to one another. Gutjuk shares bush plums with Travis, who in turn teaches him how to use a rifle. This act of trust will have serious ramifications for both characters. Wide shots of them traversing the land frame them side by side on horseback, suggesting a growing sense of unity. However, this is not a sufficiently strong bond for Gutjuk to entirely trust Travis. When Travis probes, 'one chance to save your uncle's life … where is he?' Gutjuk is mute, possibly influenced by Claire's parting words not to trust anyone.

Several times, the two men come to each other's rescue and, when Travis is captured and disarmed by the Wild Mob, Gutjuk appeals to his uncle, concerned about Travis' welfare: 'What are you going to do with him? … he's a good man.' Even Baywara refers to him as 'your friend' when talking to his nephew. Baywara has very good reasons to be suspicious of Travis or any white man, telling his father, 'You can't trust them. You know what they did.' Yet Därrpa clearly has more faith in people, giving Travis back his rifle as a gesture of goodwill and idealistically approaching Moran in hopes of negotiating a peaceful solution.

Reuniting with his uncle represents a shift in loyalties for Gutjuk, conflicted about who to trust and who to follow. At the same time, Gulwirri treats Gutjuk's return with scepticism and suspicion, her eyes darting back to him as the Wild Mob walk to Därrpa's country. Later, when the group departs for the meeting with Moran, she cynically asks

Därrpa: 'You're going on the word of a white man and a mission boy?' Initially, Gulwirri keeps a physical distance between herself and Gutjuk, lumping him in with all men, whom she sees as weak and cowardly. But gradually she learns to trust Gutjuk, supporting him in his revenge and fighting alongside him in the film's climax.

When Travis says Gutjuk's name in one of the final lines of the film, it speaks volumes about their relationship. Over twelve years, through deception, lies, insurmountable obstacles and endless casualties, they have forged an unlikely but undeniable bond built on respect. The close-up shot of their hands, two different skin tones, clasped tightly together, signifies Johnson's own views on reconciliation. The director advocates for healing, not just in interpersonal relationships but as a nation, suggesting that without mutual trust there can be no progress or resolution.

DIFFERENT INTERPRETATIONS

Different interpretations arise from different responses to a text. Over time, a text will evoke a wide range of responses from its readers, who may come from various social or cultural groups and live in very different places and historical periods. Responses by critics and reviewers can be published in newspapers, journals and books, both online and in print. They can also be expressed in discussions among readers in the media, classrooms, book groups and so on.

While there is no single correct reading or interpretation of a text, it is important to understand that an interpretation is more than a personal opinion – it is the justification of a point of view on the text. To present an interpretation of a text based on your point of view, you must use a logical argument and support it with relevant evidence from the text.

Critical viewpoints

Although *High Ground* was favourably received by most film critics, there was some initial trepidation conveyed about a First Nations story centred around a white protagonist. However, it can convincingly be argued that it is Gutjuk, not Travis, who is the film's main character. This misunderstanding could have stemmed from the prominent images of Simon Baker being used to promote the film, perhaps a simple economic strategy from producers given Baker's reputation and Hollywood pedigree. Alternatively, the cynical inference here is that white audiences wouldn't embrace such a challenging and unsettling film without a familiar (white) face guiding them through it.

Many concerns also stemmed from a heightened awareness of the clichéd and often offensive 'white saviour' narratives seen in countless films. In these stories, a Caucasian hero or heroine is often portrayed as 'saving' non-white characters, literally or figuratively, the racist implication being that they couldn't survive without such intervention.

Although these films have always existed in Hollywood, there are many contemporary films that follow this formula, such as *Freedom Writers* (2007), *The Blind Side* (2009) and *The Help* (2011).

When *High Ground* premiered at the Berlin Film Festival in 2020, Wendy Ide of *Screen Daily* touched on this debate:

> The decision to equally foreground a white man's story might lead to some criticism, particularly as that character's actions and attitude seem as much informed by contemporary guilt and desire for reparation as they are by period accuracy. (Ide 2020)

Although massacres of First Nations people were notoriously under-reported or documented, it is reasonable to question whether Travis' actions in the film would ever have occurred during the time period or whether contemporary guilt shapes a revisionist and unlikely rendering. Prominent Australian film critic Jim Schembri espoused the revisionist interpretation: 'it's as though Travis is there to represent contemporary white guilt over the historic atrocities committed against the indigenous population' (Schembri 2021).

It wasn't only Australian reviewers who critiqued Johnson's choices. American writer Roxana Hadadi questioned whether the film's attempts to equally focus on two cultures provided a 'hint at both-sides-ism', resulting in one-dimensional portrayals:

> … the film's most obvious missteps involve how its primary characters sometimes feel more like broad types (the hesitant white man, the betrayed Indigenous boy) than like specific people. (Hadadi 2021)

Many other critics agree, referencing the underwritten role of Walter as a missed opportunity to explore the nuances of postcolonialism and provide deeper insights into the various perspectives.

Two interpretations

Interpretation 1: As Travis demonstrates, morality is complex and not always universal.

The many characters in *High Ground* display dualities and contradictions, and are subsequently difficult to categorise definitively. Johnson portrays Travis as a complicated and challenging figure who is often hard to read. Although laconic in nature, he is certainly not indifferent to the suffering he has contributed to. A loyal soldier turned police officer, he draws a line in refusing to conform to other people's dubious moral codes. Eventually, Travis is able to demonstrate his own sense of morality, more through actions than words.

Initially, Travis is assumed to be a trustworthy member of the amoral Northern Territory police. As a sniper, he is portrayed as a vital part of a horseback military-like operation sent to track down criminals accused of killing livestock. In these scenes, Travis is attired in police uniform, superficially depicted as similar to his bloodthirsty colleagues who are eager to attack – 'What are we waiting for?' Shot from a high camera angle as he crouches from on top of a rock formation ready to shoot, he is supported by Eddy, who defers to Travis' expertise; Eddy decrees, 'nobody shoots but him', pointing upwards to Travis.

Johnson's use of a subjective, point-of-view shot through Travis' rifle crosshairs as he stalks and hunts an innocent clan deliberately depicts him as part of the problem, a threatening and predatory presence. The diegetic sound of Travis' heavy breathing as he moves his rifle from potential target to potential target, reinforced by his first lines of 'I'm here, Eddy', suggests that he is ready and willing to perpetuate the impending violence. Contributing to the idea of duty, Johnson portrays Travis as a World War I veteran who fought alongside Eddy, gaining a reputation as a skilful marksman. Moran even reminds Travis, later, that 'we got through the war by sticking together', reinforcing the initial indication that Travis is a loyal and duty-bound soldier, now voluntarily working within a corrupt and amoral police force.

However, an unexpected moment of rebellion suggests that Travis is instead loyal to his own innate sense of right and wrong. When the police operation quickly turns into a bloodbath, Travis witnesses his colleagues' glee as they inhumanely and unjustly shoot innocent women and children. Surprisingly, Travis turns his rifle on his fellow police officers instead. Thus 'two whitefellas end up with bullets in them', the actions tantamount to treason according to his superior, Moran. Later, the police captain calls him a 'mad dog' for his disloyalty, telling Travis, 'You break my heart, son.' Yet Travis refuses to be complicit in a cover-up, bluntly telling Eddy, 'I'm not lyin'' when asked to 'act as a unit'. When Eddy attempts to downplay the fact that he fired first – 'What does it matter?' – Travis very firmly tells him 'it matters', reinforcing his own sense of morality and righteousness. Travis' revulsion at his complicity is clear from his shame-filled facial expressions and downcast stare, and reinforced by Johnson's use of multiple close-up shots. After Claire slaps him it is clear that he shares her disgust, taking the slap as a form of penance and not even attempting to refute her. Although his departure from the police force could be seen as somewhat selfish and cowardly, as he does nothing to ensure that justice is served, his feelings of guilt are never far from the surface. He is perceived by those lacking integrity as disloyal, but it is apparent Travis has the moral 'high ground' over many of his peers.

Ultimately, Travis' actions demonstrate his morality and he eventually finds partial redemption for his troubled past. Vowing to Eddy that he 'won't make the same mistake twice', Travis reveals his own principles and ideas about justice, intent on a long-overdue righting of his wrongs. In ensuring the young Gutjuk, during the massacre, is not another innocent casualty of police brutality, Travis establishes a connection to the young First Nations boy that will have significant repercussions twelve years later. Although Travis keeps most of his emotions and motivations hidden, his actions speak louder than words. On multiple occasions he rescues Gutjuk from the hands of a sadistic and savage Eddy, such as at the mission when he snaps, 'Leave it Eddy! Leave it!', pushing his former colleague to the ground and tussling with him in the outback dust. Knowing the harsh realities of the Frontier Wars, Travis teaches Gutjuk how to use his rifle, telling him, 'You should probably learn to shoot.' As such, he inadvertently equips the boy with the tools and the skills to enact his long-overdue revenge. In the denouement of the film, Travis steps into the line of fire to prevent Gutjuk being killed, a moment that explicitly reveals his shifted loyalties from his former colleagues to Gutjuk's safety and wellbeing. Although it took twelve years, Travis demonstrates he does have sense of morality after all.

Interpretation 2: *High Ground* shows there is more than one form of heroism.

The 'high ground' in the film's title refers to the literal position a sniper employs when getting ready to fire. More symbolically, the director also hints at a moral 'high ground' – a figurative space reserved for those characters who act virtuously and courageously. There are multiple characters who act heroically and admirably in the film, at various times and for various reasons. Although Travis may be established as courageous initially and cursorily, Gutjuk, Gulwirri and Claire act with much more conviction, humanity and bravery, and as such are the true heroes of *High Ground*.

Travis is not the hero of the film, although he has moments of courage and, when juxtaposed with his brutal and racist colleagues in the Northern Territory police force, he emerges as the most principled of his kind. Despite wearing a police uniform, Travis is portrayed as distant and detached from his colleagues. He is shown at the beginning of the film in a physically higher position than those on the ground, to symbolically represent the divide. Travis first avenges the death of Gutjuk's mother, then protects the boy from the clutches of the murderous officers, delivering him into the safer hands of Claire at the East Alligator River Mission. Later, he intervenes when Eddy becomes physically threatening, ensuring Gutjuk's safety once more. And in the final stages of the film, Travis steps in front of an oncoming bullet to save the lives of others.

In addition to his physical acts of valour, he also refuses to help cover up the massacre – 'I'm not lyin'' – and earns the scorn of his racist and corrupt contemporaries.

But *High Ground* is essentially Gutjuk's tale and Johnson portrays him as the heart and soul of the film: a courageous and humane character. Gutjuk's core attributes are established in childhood, as within the film's prologue Johnson portrays him as eager to learn the customs of his clan, with his father predicting his eventual success: 'One day your time will come to be a hunter.' After enduring the unspeakable and horrific injustice of his family's murders, Gutjuk admirably keeps his trauma and inevitable resentments hidden. The adult Gutjuk has had his identity stripped away and his name changed, yet he still interacts with white Australians respectfully and obediently, referring to others as 'Sir' and showing Eddy and Travis more mercy and tolerance than they deserve.

Gutjuk's true courage and heroism emerges when he decides to avenge the deaths of his kin, a quiet and dutiful 'mission boy' no longer. Although he brandishes a rifle and bandoliers, he never indiscriminately kills another, despite multiple opportunities to do so. This sets Gutjuk apart from every other character in the film and demonstrates his true humanity. A flashback to his childhood before he embarks on his own revenge suggests that he has managed to come full circle with his identity and culture, despite the adversity he has experienced. Johnson employs low camera angles of a warrior-like Gutjuk, bravely fighting back after years of keeping quiet. Wearing the white ochre markings of his clan in part as tribute and partly as warpaint, Johnson highlights Gutjuk's new-found defiance and fearlessness: 'You killed my family! Say it!' Despite this, Gutjuk also demonstrates true empathy and kindness by staying with Travis until he dies, firmly clasping the very hand that contributed to the massacre of his family. Johnson concludes the film with a fading shot of a soaring hawk, Gutjuk's namesake, to symbolically reinforce who the true hero of his film is.

If Gutjuk might be considered the central hero of the film, Gulwirri and Claire are its unsung heroines. Although marginalised by their male counterparts, both exhibit impressive courage and bravery, taking a stand against injustice. Gulwirri is fearless and unapologetic, joining the Wild Mob, a vigilante group of renegades who refuse to kowtow to those who stole their land. Even so, she is not reticent about voicing her dissent to her male counterparts, rebuking them for their perceived incompetence: 'You don't know what you're doing. You're all weak. Cowards … You don't speak for me.' Johnson frames her speech from a low camera angle as she stands, spear in hand, on the precipice of a cliff, affording her the 'high ground'. When she is savagely attacked by a group of white men, her brave response has a powerful impact. Knowing a racist Commonwealth justice system would never seek to reprimand her rapists, she takes matters into her own hands to ensure they are punished and can never hurt another. In a reversal of stereotypical gender roles, she commands Gutjuk to turn his head – 'don't watch' – as she turns the men's savagery back onto them. Like Gutjuk, Gulwirri has survived the massacre of her family, in addition to the unspeakable violence, abuse and exploitation of working at a station where the 'boss man thought he owned me'. Johnson imbues Gulwirri's character with true pathos and humanity, when she profoundly confesses that 'I know how it feels to be beaten'. Despite the never-ending adversity she has experienced, her courage never falters.

Similarly, Claire is not afraid of reprimanding male characters whom she feels lack decency, harshly slapping Travis across the face when learning of his complicity in the massacre: 'You were supposed to be in charge.' Although she regularly voices her concerns, her smug male counterparts rarely take her objections seriously. In the denouement of the film, she takes matters into her own hands, shooting Eddy in the heart and ending his cruel and racist vendetta. Gulwirri and Claire share a moment of recognition in the final moments of the film, with Johnson juxtaposing their close-ups as they make eye contact. Although their experiences diverge vastly, they share an unspoken kinship, each reluctantly but heroically resorting to violence to, ironically, prevent more violence.

QUESTIONS & ANSWERS

This section focuses on your own analytical writing on the text, and gives you strategies for producing high-quality responses in your coursework and exam essays.

Essay writing – an overview

An essay on a literary work is a formal and serious piece of writing that presents your point of view on the text, usually in response to a given topic. Your 'point of view' in an essay is your interpretation of the meaning of the text's language, structure, characters, situations and events, supported by detailed analysis of textual evidence.

Analyse – don't summarise

In your essays it is important to avoid simply summarising what happens in a text.

- A **summary** is a description or paraphrase (retelling in different words) of the characters and events. For example: 'Macbeth has a horrifying vision of a dagger dripping with blood before he goes to murder King Duncan'.
- An **analysis** is an explanation of the real meaning or significance that lies 'beneath' the text's words (and images, for a film). For example: 'Macbeth's vision of a bloody dagger shows how deeply uneasy he is about the violent act he is contemplating, and conveys his sense that supernatural forces are impelling him to act'.

A limited amount of summary is sometimes necessary to let your reader know which part of the text you wish to discuss. However, always keep this to a minimum and follow it immediately with your analysis of what this part of the text is really telling us.

Plan your essay

Carefully plan your essay so that you have a clear idea of what you are going to say. The plan ensures that your ideas flow logically, that your argument remains consistent and that you stay on the topic. An essay plan should be a list of **brief dot points** covering no more than half a page.

- Include your central argument or main contention – a concise statement of your overall response to the topic.
- Write three or four dot points for each paragraph, indicating the main idea and evidence/examples from the text. Note that in your essay you will need to *expand* on these points and *analyse* the evidence.

Structure your essay

An essay is a complete, self-contained piece of writing. It has a clear beginning (the introduction), middle (several body paragraphs) and end (the last paragraph or conclusion). It must also have a central argument that runs throughout, linking each paragraph to form a coherent whole. See examples of introductions and conclusions in the 'Analysing a sample topic' and 'Sample answer' sections.

The introduction establishes your overall response to the topic. It includes your main contention and outlines the main evidence you will refer to in the course of the essay. Write your introduction *after* you have done a plan and *before* you write the rest of the essay.

The body paragraphs argue your case – they present evidence from the text and explain how this evidence supports your argument. Each body paragraph needs:

- a strong **topic sentence** (usually the first sentence) that states the main point being made in the paragraph
- **evidence** from the text, including some brief quotations
- **analysis** of the textual evidence, with **explanation** of its significance and how it supports your argument
- **links back to the topic** in one or more statements, usually towards the end of the paragraph.

Connect the body paragraphs so that your discussion flows smoothly. Use some linking words and phrases such as 'similarly' and 'on the other hand', though don't start every paragraph like this. Another strategy is to use a significant word from the last sentence of one paragraph in the first sentence of the next.

Use key terms from the topic – or synonyms for them – throughout, so the relevance of your discussion to the topic is always clear.

The conclusion ties everything together and finishes the essay. It includes strong statements that emphasise your central argument and provide a clear response to the topic.

Avoid simply restating the points made earlier in the essay – this will end on a very flat note and imply that you have run out of ideas and vocabulary. The conclusion should be a logical extension of what you have written, not just a repetition or summary of it. Writing an effective conclusion can be a challenge. Try using these tips:

- Start by linking back to the final sentence of the second-last paragraph, rather than leaping to your main contention straight away – this helps your writing to flow.
- Use synonyms and expressions with equivalent meanings to vary your vocabulary. This allows you to reinforce your line of argument without being repetitive.
- When planning your essay, think of one or two broad statements or observations about the text's wider meaning. These should be related to the topic and your overall argument. Keep them for the conclusion, since they will give you something 'new' to say but still follow logically from your discussion. The introduction will be focused on the topic, but the conclusion can present a wider view of the text.

Essay topics

1. What is the significance of the title of Johnson's film?
2. '*High Ground* suggests that some conflicts can never be resolved.' Discuss.
3. "He needs to learn his place."
   What does Gutjuk learn over the course of the film?
4. How does Johnson use film techniques to explore the idea of justice in *High Ground*?
5. 'The characters in *High Ground* keep their true motivations hidden.' Do you agree?
6. How is violence used differently by the characters in Johnson's film?
7. "You can't share a country."
   '*High Ground* is a scathing indictment of Australia's colonial history.' Discuss.
8. 'Revenge comes at a cost.' How does *High Ground* explore this idea?
9. 'The importance of trust and loyalty is the core of this film.' Do you agree?
10. 'The female characters in *High Ground* are more principled than the men.'
    To what extent do you agree?

Vocabulary for writing on *High Ground*

Aerial shot: cinematographic style; filmed from the air (also known as a drone shot).

Cinematography: the art of capturing images on film.

Denouement: the final unravelling and resolution of the plot.

Diegetic sound: sound that exists within the world of the film.

First Nations: referring to Aboriginal and Torres Strait Islander peoples and their cultures.

Juxtaposition: in film, the editing of two or more shots to create a certain effect, idea or contrast.

Linear structure: a narrative structure in which events are presented chronologically.

Mise en scène: a French term meaning 'scene setting', encompassing all the visual elements within the frame – actors, locations, sets, costumes, props and lighting.

Motif: a recurring image, symbol or theme.

Postcolonial: relating to a period following colonialism; in the Australian context, this is generally considered to be the period after Federation in 1901.

Totem: a symbol of an individual's ancestral spirit, often in the form of an animal.

Yolngu Matha: meaning 'Yolngu tongue' or 'Yolngu language'; the family of languages spoken by First Nations people in Arnhem Land.

Analysing a sample topic

'The characters in *High Ground* keep their true motivations hidden.' Do you agree?

This question invites you to consider challenging the topic. You may choose to agree, disagree or partly agree. In this case, partly disagreeing may allow you to show a broader understanding of the text. Ensure your contention is clear in the introduction, and justify it clearly. You could start by asking yourself questions in order to help form this contention. Below are some examples.

- Key words in the topic are 'true motivations' and 'hidden' – how do you define these terms? What synonyms could you substitute to avoid sounding repetitive? What are antonyms for these terms?
- Does the idea of a 'true' motivation suggest some degree of duplicity, deceit or strategy?

- Which characters are not revealing their real agendas and why?
- If true motivations are 'hidden', how do we know what they are? What clues or hints do we see?
- What are the consequences of concealment? Does it breed tension, intrigue, conflict?
- Does this change? Are characters' true motivations revealed by the end of the film?

The following is one way to tackle this topic. However, there is no one 'correct' interpretation here. As long as you explicitly address the topic and link all your arguments and evidence back to it, there are multiple approaches you could take. In this case, it may be easier to focus on one character at a time.

Sample introduction

> 'He knows more than he's letting on ...'. In Stephen Johnson's revisionist Western film, *High Ground*, most of the characters attempt to keep their true feelings and motivations concealed. The reasons for this are varied and complex: distrust, strategy and duplicity are some of the rationales for their reticence. As a result of this, characters doubt and misunderstand one another, leading to rising conflict and tension. However, by the denouement of the film, as these conflicting interests and motives intersect, all pretence is abandoned and true feelings are forced to the surface.

Body paragraph outline

Paragraph 1: Travis unsuccessfully attempts to keep his feelings of guilt and resentment hidden.

- Despite quitting the police force and attempting to get on with his life, it is clear Travis has unfinished business.
- Although Travis agrees to help track down Baywara, his reluctance and the revulsion he feels for Moran and Eddy are clear.

→

- Asked by both Claire and Gutjuk what his true intentions are, his responses are vague, e.g. 'I'm not going to make it easy'.
- Travis never apologises to Gutjuk or takes any responsibility for his role in the massacre, yet his actions reveal his real allegiances: he kills several of his colleagues, rescues Gutjuk from harm several times and sacrifices his life for others, finally showing his decency and loyalty.

Paragraph 2: Although Gutjuk presents himself as a dutiful 'mission boy', he harbours secret loyalties and plans for revenge.

- Tommy initially follows orders, and is polite and compliant.
- However, private conversations reveal he may have a hidden agenda: 'They went for it'.
- Travis is able to see through this facade: 'He knows more than he's letting on'.
- Despite Travis and Gutjuk concealing their true intentions, they manage to bond and learn to trust one another.
- In the climax of the film, Gutjuk's true self is reclaimed; his repressed anger rises to the surface as he avenges the wrongs done to him and his family.

Paragraph 3: Eddy and Moran hide behind their positions of authority but their shameless racism is soon exposed.

- Eddy tries to conceal the true story of the massacre.
- Eddy's racism, vengeance and desire to dominate is later revealed: 'You can't share a country'.
- Moran prides himself on duty; via his staging of official photographs he attempts to present an image of formality.
- When alone with Travis, Moran reveals to him that he unapologetically considers himself a 'bad' man.

Sample conclusion

High Ground portrays conflicting and conflicted characters, each with their own private driving force. Despite a desire to keep their true motivations hidden, the rising tensions that result force emotions to erupt and true colours to be revealed. Some characters are exposed as virtuous and loyal with an admirable quest for justice. Others are exposed as cruel, sadistic and unrepentant, and ultimately suffer harsh consequences as a result.

SAMPLE ANSWER

How is violence used differently by different characters in Johnson's film?

In the 2020 'Meat Pie' Western film *High Ground*, director Stephen Maxwell Johnson portrays a brutal, violent and deliberately confronting postcolonial Australia. Although senseless slaughter, perpetual retaliation and constant threats of more brutality fill almost every frame, Johnson depicts a clear distinction between his characters in terms of how and why each resorts to violence. Some employ it as a tool to dominate, strike terror and settle old scores. Others turn violence back onto their tormentors, empowering themselves in the process. Although Johnson condemns those who revel in sadism, he is more sympathetic to those who resort to physical force when they have few options left.

Initially, violence is depicted as a means for those in positions of authority to terrorise and control others. In his deliberately confronting and unflinching depictions of carnage in the early scenes, Johnson portrays the Northern Territory police inflicting sadistic and unjustifiable 'chaos' on a group of innocent First Nations people, a massacre that leaves 'seventeen dead'. These scenes are particularly unsettling as we watch unsuspecting women and children frolic and prepare food in an ominous point-of-view shot through police sniper Travis' rifle crosshairs. Ironically, his colleague Eddy says just before the attack that they 'don't want any trouble', which is immediately contradicted by another impatient police officer asking, 'What are we waiting for?', suggesting that they are eager and willing to ambush the unsuspecting group. Johnson incorporates chilling mid-shots of women cradling babies in huts that provide no protection from the police rifles. Subsequent shots of police firing at the backs of clan members as they try to flee portray senseless violence that some even treat as sport. 'Did I get her?' one police officer gleefully asks after he kills a woman. In the aftermath of the massacre, the police officers are 'haunted' by their actions, not in regret, but because of the 'mess' of leaving behind eyewitnesses; 'I don't need to tell you what happens if this Baywara gets a voice', police captain Moran warns. Even years later, his officer, Eddy, continues to threaten or shoot anyone who dares question or challenge him, physically assaulting Gutjuk with the menacing words, 'tell me what you know … and I might let you breathe again'.

Johnson also portrays European civilians resorting to violence as a means of terrorising First Nations people. Gulwirri is sexually assaulted by a laughing group of 'whitefellas', and this is not the first time she has experienced sexual violence at the hands of men in authority. Later, she reveals that she experienced similar assaults as a young girl working at a station: 'Boss man thought he owned me … he gave me to his men.' Johnson unequivocally condemns this type of violence, perpetrated by cruel, unrepentant and domineering colonialists on innocent people.

However, some characters see violence as the only form of justice available to them. When Baywara survives the massacre that kills his family, none of the perpetrators face any repercussions, despite later appeals to authorities to 'give us our justice for the man who killed my family'. Refusing to be terrorised, Baywara forms a vigilante group of his own, nicknamed the Wild Mob, who decide to take back their stolen land from European colonisers by 'wreaking havoc, killing livestock, burning stations'. This form of payback blurs revenge with justice but serves to empower and embolden Baywara. He channels his anger into violence, unafraid of retaliation, declaring that if people are sent after him, he will 'send them back ghosts'. Johnson implies that Baywara saw no other options available, that he never 'had a chance' to be 'a different kind of man'. This suggests that there is a continual cycle of violence that can occur when victims become offenders themselves. This is also seen in the sexual assault of Gulwirri. Her rapists ignore her guttural screams for mercy, instead laughing in her face and denigrating her as a 'stupid bitch'. Gulwirri's response is to become violent herself, brutally and mercilessly beating the men to death. Knowing her actions are horrific but seeing no other choice, she says to Gutjuk 'don't watch' as she finishes the job. Like Baywara, she refuses to be victimised and terrorised, using violence only as a last resort. Johnson sympathises with the victims of violence who see justice denied and see physical retaliation as their only recourse.

The film also portrays characters using violence to take a courageous and moral stand. This idea is first established via Travis' sudden rebellion during the massacre, as a result of which 'two whitefellas end up with [his] bullets in them'. Travis, horrified by the brutality of his fellow police officers, takes a solitary but principled stand in shooting his colleagues. Although this is seen as an act of betrayal by his fellow police officers, who label Travis a 'problem' with 'no sense of loyalty' and 'a mad dog', Johnson does not condemn this type of violence. Drawing on the tropes of traditional Western films, Travis' actions highlight a temporary triumph of good over evil. In the denouement of the film, another unexpected but righteous act of violence is similarly rationalised. As Eddy continues to terrorise, pulling his gun on Travis and Gutjuk, threatening the latter with, 'say goodbye, you black bastard', the reign of terror, manifest here in the deadly stand-off, is aborted with a sole bullet fired by Claire. Marginalised for much of the film, Claire is depicted here as emerging from the literal margins of the frame, having just pulled the trigger on the loathsome Eddy. As her beloved church burns in the background, Claire draws upon the biblical idea of 'an eye for an eye' to justify the punishment of those seen to deserve it. Like Travis and Gulwirri before her, Claire takes no pleasure in her use of violence, but deems it a necessary action to suppress more evil.

Although an explicitly violent film, *High Ground* is also a moral film. Johnson paints a clear distinction between characters who revel in violence and those who use it with ostensible justification. Exploring the intent behind violence is key in ascertaining who has the moral 'high ground' and who is deserving of condemnation.

REFERENCES & READING

Text

High Ground 2020, dir. Stephen Maxwell Johnson, Madman Films. Starring Jacob Junior Nayinggul and Simon Baker.

Books

Reynolds, H 2000, *Why Weren't We Told? A Personal Search for the Truth About our History*, Melbourne University Publishing, Melbourne.

Reynolds, H 1990, *With the White People*, Penguin Books, Melbourne.

Reviews

Hadadi, R 2021, 'Review: *High Ground*', *RogerEbert.com*, 14 May, https://www.rogerebert.com/reviews/high-ground-movie-review-2021

Ide, W 2020, '*High Ground*': Berlin Review, *Screen Daily*, 24 February, https://www.screendaily.com/reviews/high-ground-berlin-review/5147533.article

Schembri, J 2021, 'An earnest film about our dark past, *High Ground* suffers from white-guilt cliches, thin plotting and too much virtue signalling', *JimSchembri.com*, 4 February, https://www.jimschembri.com/an-earnest-film-about-our-dark-past-high-ground-suffers-from-white-guilt-cliches-thin-plotting-and-too-much-virtue-signalling/

Websites

Australian Government Style Manual 2022, 'Aboriginal and Torres Strait Islander peoples', https://www.stylemanual.gov.au/accessible-and-inclusive-content/inclusive-language/aboriginal-and-torres-strait-islander-peoples

Chang, C 2019, 'How early Australians treated Aboriginal people', *News.com.au*, 21 January, https://www.news.com.au/national/politics/how-early-australians-treated-aboriginal-people/news-story/e984d3a453382c59a1d5d81f99a9ad8c

Charles Darwin University 2014, *Yolngu dictionary*, https://yolngudictionary.cdu.edu.au/Word_search.php

Cunningham, J 2021, 'Andrew Comis ACS on Filming *High Ground*', *Australian Cinematographer*, https://acmag.com.au/2021/01/01/high-ground/

Dhimurru Aboriginal Corporation, 'Yolngu culture', https://www.dhimurru.com.au/yolngu-culture.html

Korff, J, 'Appropriate words & terminology for First Nations topics', *Creative Spirits*, https://www.creativespirits.info/aboriginalculture/media/appropriate-terminology-for-aboriginal-topics#:~:text=First%20Nations%20is%20used%20worldwide,First%20Nations%20people%20in%20Australia

Milner, J 2021, 'Q&A with Stephen Maxwell Johnson', National Film and Sound Archive of Australia, https://www.nfsa.gov.au/latest/deep-dive-qa-high-ground-director-stephen-maxwell-johnson

Rademaker, L, Gumurdul, JN & May, SK 2021, 'How historically accurate is the film *High Ground*? The violence it depicts is uncomfortably close to the truth', *The Conversation*, 10 February, https://theconversation.com/how-historically-accurate-is-the-film-high-ground-the-violence-it-depicts-is-uncomfortably-close-to-the-truth-154475

University of Newcastle 2022, *Colonial Frontier Massacres, Australia, 1788 to 1930*, https://c21ch.newcastle.edu.au/colonialmassacres/map.php